GODS AND OTHER ODD CREATURES
As the Greeks and Romans Saw Them

Other Books By Rose Williams

Going to Hades is Easy
(Issued as Latin Quips at your Fingertips)

Once Upon the Tiber

The Lighter Side of the Dark Ages

The Labors of Aeneas

Cicero the Patriot

GODS AND OTHER ODD CREATURES
As the Greeks and Romans Saw Them

I retell ancient poets' monstrous lies.   Ovid *Amores III*, 6. 17

This tale and similar legends about the gods I relate
without believing them, but I relate them nevertheless.
Pausanias, *Description of Greece II.17.5*

By Rose Williams
Illustrated by James Hillyer Estes

Published By

CicadaSun

Copyright © 2007 by Rose Williams

All rights reserved. No part of this book may be reproduced, utilized or transmitted in any form, or by means of any technology now known or unknown, without prior permission in writing from the Publisher except for inclusion in brief quotations in a review. Inquiries should be addressed to: CicadaSun, P.O. Box 90834, Austin, Texas 78709-0834

Published by CicadaSun
Austin, Texas
www.cicadasun.com

Printed in USA

Book design and production by CicadaSun

Publisher's Cataloging-in-Publication
(Provided by Quality Books, Inc.)

Williams, Rose, 1937-
  Gods and other odd creatures : as the Greeks and
Romans saw them / by Rose Williams ; illustrations by
James Hillyer Estes.
    p. cm.
  Includes bibliographical references and index.
  LCCN 2007936326
  ISBN-13: 978-0-9779808-1-9
  ISBN-10: 0-9779808-1-2

  1. Classical, Mythology. 2. Gods, Greek. 3. Gods, Roman. 4. Greece--Religious life and customs. 5. Rome --Religious life and customs. I. Title.

BL723.W55 2008   292.1'3
                       QBI07-600256

Preface

When dealing with Greco-Roman mythology one must take into account the ambivalent attitude, and often the patent disbelief, openly expressed by many prominent members of both societies, including the two quoted above who are engaged in telling the stories. In the First Punic War the Roman commander Publius Claudius Pulcher, on being informed that a sea battle could not be fought because the sacred chickens would not eat, threw them into the sea and said, "Then let them drink." (Cicero, *De Natura Deorum, II, 7*). Cato the Censor always wondered how two haruspices (members of a college of priestly soothsayers) could look at each other without laughing. (Cicero, *De Divinatione, II, 51*). However, in *De Divinatione II 148-150* Cicero says that it is proper for a wise man to keep the rituals, ceremonies, and customs of his ancestors, but to keep religion and superstition separated.[1] Much thought and philosophical discussion was expended in the attempts to achieve this balance. These struggles in no way lessened the impact of the gods, their festivals and holy places, and their temples upon classical daily life and practices.

Consideration must also be given to the nature of the classical deities. They were often jealous, petty and unfair, but must be propitiated at all costs. Throughout the *Aeneid* Aeneas, the Trojan warrior and legendary ancestor of the Romans, is constantly pursued by the unyielding hatred of the great Queen of Heaven, Juno. There is never any intimation that Aeneas has done wrong or even shown any *lese majeste* toward Juno; she just doesn't like Trojans, and he is one -- and a strong leader of them, at that. He constantly makes offerings to her without making any impression upon her until Jupiter tells her flatly that she might as well give in, as the Fates, much more powerful than any god, have given Aeneas a destiny that she cannot subvert.

Thus classical mythology should not be approached with the deadly seriousness usually connected with the great religions of the modern day. This little book attempts to convey both the amused and tolerant attitude toward the gods and the great importance given to their place in society.

The gods use us mortals as footballs.
Plautus, *Captivi, Prologus, 22*

The wrath of the gods may be great, but it certainly is slow.
Juvenal, *Satirae, 100*

Table of Contents

Introduction	1
Part I - The Gods	4
Chapter I - How Things Came to Be	4
Chapter II - Elder Gods	6
1. A. Cronus	7
B. Roman/Saturn	7
2. Rhea/ Roman Ops	8
3. Iapetus	9
4. Oceanus	9
5. Tethys	9
6. Atlas	9
7. Prometheus	10
8. Epimetheus	10
Chapter III - Olympians and/or Dii Consentes	13
1. A. Zeus, King of Gods and Father of Men	15
B. Roman Jupiter	18
2. A. Hera, Queen of the Gods	19
B. Roman Juno	23
3. A. Poseidon, God of the Sea	24
B. Roman Neptune, God of Waters	26
4. A. Pluto/Hades, God of the Underworld	27
B. Roman Pluto	31
5. A. Hestia, Goddess of the Hearth	31
B. Roman Vesta	33
6. A. Athena, Goddess of Wisdom	34
B. Roman Minerva	36
7. A. Phoebus Apollo, God of the Sun	36
B. Roman Apollo	41
C. Mithras	41

8. A. Artemis, Goddess of the Moon and Hunting	43
B. Roman Diana	45
9. A. Aphrodite, Goddess of Love	46
B. Roman Venus	51
10. A. Ares, God of War	52
B. Roman Mars	54
11. A. Hermes, Messenger God	55
B. Roman Mercury	58
12. A. Hephaestus, God of Fire and Forge	59
B. Roman Vulcan	61
Chapter IV - The Great Earth Gods	63
1. A. Demeter, Goddess of Agriculture	63
B. Roman Ceres	65
C. Cybele	66
2. A. Dionysus, God of Wine	67
B. Roman Liber/Bacchus	71
Chapter V- Uniquely Roman Deities	72
1. Dii Consentes	72
2. Dii Familiaris	72
A. Lares	72
B. Penates	72
C. Genius and Juno	73
3. Janus, God of Doors	73
Part II Temples and Festivals of the Gods	75
Section I. Elder Gods	75
1. A. Temples and Festivals of Cronus and Rhea	75
B. Temples and Festivals of Saturn	76
Section II. Olympians	77
1. A. Temples of Zeus	77
B. Temples of Jupiter	80
2. A. Temples of Hera	81
B. Temples of Juno	83
3. A. Temples of Poseidon	83
B. Temples of Neptune	84
4. A. Temples of Pluto	86
B. Temple of Roman Pluto	86

5. A. Temples of Hestia ... 87
   B Temples of Vesta ... 87
6. A. Temples of Athena ... 90
   B. Temples of Minerva ... 91
7. A. Temples of Apollo ... 92
   B. Temples of Roman Apollo ... 93
   C. Temples of Mithras ... 95
8. A. Temples of Artemis ... 95
   B. Temples of Diana ... 98
9. A. Temples of Aphrodite ... 99
   B. Temples of Venus ... 99
10. A. Temple of Ares ... 100
    B. Temple of Mars ... 101
11. A. Temple of Hermes ... 101
    B. Temple of Mercury ... 102
12. A. Temples of Hephaestus In Athens ... 103
    B. Temple of Vulcan ... 103

Section III. Great Earth Gods ... 105
1. A. Temple of Demeter ... 105
   B. Temple of Ceres ... 106
2. A. Temple of Dionysus ... 110
   B a. Temple of Liber ... 110
   B b. Temple of Bacchus ... 111

Section IV Temples and Festivals of Uniquely Roman Deities ... 112
1. Shrine to the Genius of the Roman People ... 112
2. Temple of Janus ... 112

Notes ... 115
Appendix I ... 124
Index ... 126

Introduction

The trouble with the classical Greco-Roman deities is that, even though they have been defunct for at least fifteen hundred years, we can't pin them down. The inhabitants of peninsular and insular Greece, as well as those of Asia Minor, had a mosaic of city-states great and small, and each of these had its own idea of the gods. The Romans sailed merrily into this cultural chaos and adopted the stories at random, picking and choosing and adding their own interpretations as they saw fit. They then proceeded to give the gods they chose another set of names. (This was totally unnecessary – most of them had several already, due to the Greeks' having carried out the same process when they arrived in the Mediterranean area). The new names were those of established Roman and Etruscan gods (most of whom were no doubt scandalized by the shocking qualities now attributed to them; they had been a staid and rather dull set of totems until all those Greek stories came along).

Religions of all sorts are constantly impacted by what happens to the societies that practice them, and classical paganism as viewed from the modern world resembles a badly fractured mosaic. From the latter part of the nineteenth century onward, various scholars hoped to bring some order to the general chaos by examining the origins of the gods. They rummaged around in the very early Mediterranean societies that preceded the Greeks. This rummaging wasn't very easy, as written records of that period are few to none, and such conclusions as they drew from archeology and artifacts have been proposed, debunked, and reproposed right down to the present day. Some of these scholars proclaimed that the early societies were matriarchal in character. Even Will Durant mentions coyly that various early societies, such as that of Egypt, had matriarchal qualities, especially in the realm of inheritance, as goods, chattels, and that the right to be pharaoh descended through the female line. Robert Graves went so far as to say, "Ancient Europe had no gods." (*The Greek Myths: I, p. 13*). He went on to state that it had only one goddess, the Great Mother Earth, though she appeared in a dazzling array of forms. This Great Mother Goddess had many different names and pictorial representations, most of which looked like they could benefit from a series of visits to a weight clinic. She also had a disconcerting way of appearing as a female of varying ages, sometimes a maiden, sometimes a matron, and sometimes an old hag, so that matters are complicated still further as the prototypes of Artemis/Diana, Aphrodite/Venus and Gaia/Rhea wind up as three faces of the same deity. (Athena/Minerva and Hera/Juno also double up according to this theory as maiden and crone respectively, but prudent souls should think twice before lightly announcing that Hera was a crone or that Athena was anything she might take amiss).

In this era, time was reckoned by the moon, which makes very obvious changes in short order and comes back as strong as ever in a cycle of twenty-eight days. The sun, which dawdles around for a quarter of a year or more before doing anything easily observable and then weakens pitifully for a long stretch, wasn't considered in the earliest times very useful for making day to day calculations, though nice for getting a tan in summer and spotting enemies any time of the year. The moon, on the other hand, went through that dramatic aging process once every 28 days, and some poetic souls proclaimed that its three life cycles were a representation of the Great Mother, who could be maiden, matron, and old hag. A little later, the Archaic Matriarch was also compared to the seasons: she was a maiden in spring, a nymph in summer, a matron in autumn, and it was back to haghood again for winter. By this time, the sun was getting a little respect, as the moon alone could not account for the seasons.

Since the concept of human fatherhood had not been discovered, the Great Mother and her earthly representative, the Priestess/Queen, had everything their own way and ruled the roost, making use of the masculine contingent as lovers, warriors, and sacrifices. Even in those early days men were somewhat larger than women (though evidently up to this point certainly not smarter), so no doubt they also had such privileges as finishing off enemies, getting things down off high shelves and opening stubborn jars. One of the finest of their number also had the very doubtful privilege of marrying the Queen and being King for a Year, at the end of which he was sacrificed and another was chosen in his stead. As enlightenment concerning fatherhood slowly dawned on these people, the men gained a greater foothold on power. The cities, however, still worshipped goddesses and perhaps served all-powerful queens.

Whatever unending squabbles rage over the theory outlined above, there seems to be fairly general agreement that goddess-worshipping societies around the Mediterranean were overrun by waves of Indo-European invaders from the North (called for simplicity's sake the Hellenes) who were patriarchal with a vengeance. These people had gods, big, tough gods, and they were listening to no nonsense about a world ruled by a supreme female deity with a split personality or even a whole legion of female deities. But, they found, as many invaders of later vintage have discovered, that religion is much harder than political power to uproot. They wound up juxtaposing each of their gods to a major goddess as her superior. Thus Hera/Juno acquired her husband Zeus/Jupiter, Artemis/Diana her twin brother Apollo, and Aphrodite/Venus got both an ugly husband Hephaestus/Vulcan, and a handsome but bone-headed lover Ares/Mars. Athena/Minerva remained a solitary maiden, but she was now reportedly born, by a singularly unlikely process, from the brain of Zeus/Jupiter. Hestia/Vesta, the hearth goddess, wound up the sister of Zeus/Jupiter, Poseidon/Neptune, and Pluto/Hades, and (in Greece, at least) was generally relegated to the background until somebody needed a household fire. Until the end of the classical period, however, many great cities, such as Athena's Athens, had a female head divinity.

Gods and goddesses could now be classified as chthonic, or earth deities, and Olympian, or sky deities. Romantic souls proceeded to picture the chthonic deities as female, emanating from Mother Earth and concerned with religion and the producing, protecting, and nurturing of young things, vegetation, and indeed all life. The said romantics then pictured the Olympian deities as male, emanating from the conquering sky gods and concerned with political rule and conquest.

Like so many neatly built systems, this one soon manifested a crack or two. Zeus/Jupiter, obviously an Olympian and a sky god, fitted the pattern neatly, but his two more or less co-equal brothers, Poseidon/Neptune of the sea and Pluto/Hades of the world of the dead, were definitely chthonian, if the term means on, of, or under the earth. Having established the fact that the deities are problematic, many-faced, and apt to take embarrassing turns we never expected, let us move briskly into that melting pot known as Classical Mythology.

Part I - The Gods

Chapter I - How Things Came to Be

As might be expected from what we have said so far, the Greeks and Romans had varying ideas of how things came to be, and various schools of thought clung to their own version with a tenacity worthy of twenty-first century folk who are convinced that they have religious and philosophical truth in a bottle and that everyone else should accept their version or take the consequences in this world and the next.

Most agreed that the first existence was Chaos, from which sprang one or more living beings. We will try to follow fairly closely Hesiod's *Theogony*; at least he has the advantages of having lived among the early Greeks and having tried to organize a set of stories and beliefs which was already unwieldy.

Hesiod starts with Chaos, and has Night and Erebus (the deep underworld) springing from it. Night bore Light and Day from union with Erebus (this was surely the first miracle, and says very little for inherited characteristics). Then for no apparent reason (this whole treatise is lamentably short on reason), Earth (Gaia) appears and gives birth to Heaven (Ouranos), "to cover her on every side, and to be an ever-sure abiding-place for the blessed gods." (*The Theogony, l. 121-123*). While still in productive mode, Gaia produced hills (and naturally their concomitant valleys) and some deep waters Hesiod refers to as Pontus. After this, she united with Ouranus to bear the Titans: Oceanus, Coeus and Crius, Hyperion and Iapetus, Theia and Rhea, Themis and Mnemosyne and then gold-crowned Phoebe and lovely Tethys. Last, she bore Cronos, who was wily and fierce and from the first had scant love for his starry father.

The Titans, as their name has come to suggest, were large, strong and handsome. But the genetic code sprang a leak before Mother Earth got to the next productions; they were large and strong, but failed miserably in the looks department (judging from the Renaissance viewpoint, with which the Greeks largely agreed, that man is the measure of all things.) First came the Cyclopes (the Wheel-eyed), huge and very like the Titans, except that each had only one eye, which was located in the middle of his forehead. Hesiod names them Brontes, Steropes, and Arges, but we will discover to our consternation as we go along that there are others, perhaps a hundred or so, with some appalling characteristics. Not that they were any match in appallingness, at least in appearance, for the next three, Cottus and Briareos and Gyes. These charming specimens each had one hundred arms and fifty heads, which would give pause to anyone who met one on the road. Hesiod says their strength was irresistible, but it is doubtful that anybody who met one stayed around to find out about that. Their father Ouranus, who was perhaps oversensitive, hated them from the first and hid them underground.

Mothers will be mothers, and Gaia resented this treatment of her offspring. (Besides, "underground" means in the inward parts of Mother Earth). She created a sickle of grey flint as a means of dealing with her husband's lack of fatherly feeling. She asked her children the Titans to avenge the wrongs that Ouranus had done to his other children, but all shied away except Cronus, who took the sickle and waited in ambush for his father. When Ouranus spread down to visit Gaia, Cronus cut off the parts that dangled and threw them in the sea. From Ouranus' blood came various creatures: armed Giants, Furies, and according to some accounts Aphrodite, about whom more later. Ouranus roared and attempted a retreat, (which, since he was Heaven, wasn't very successful) and vowed that his brutal son would pay for his deed when he was dethroned by a son of his own. From this point, the Titans ruled the universe for eons, but the promised downfall of Cronus was waiting in the wings, ready to pounce.

Chapter II - Elder Gods

Before we embark on our perilous retelling of these ancient stories, let us recall the warning given by Pausanias, a Greek traveler and geographer who lived around 15 CE. "The legends of Greece generally have different forms, and this is particularly true of genealogy." [Pausanias *8.53.5*]

There were untold numbers of Titans, strong, handsome, and often up to little good, but only a few need concern us.

Cronus, Father of the Gods

1. A. Cronus

First of all is Cronus (in Latin Saturn), that wily last-born who had wounded and replaced his father. He married his sister Rhea (after all, everybody he knew was a relative, as they were all children of Heaven and Earth). His bird was the golden-crested wren. When Rhea caught him with Philyra, he turned himself into a stallion and galloped off, leaving Philyra to bear the great intellectual Chiron, who was half man and half horse. (Any comparison with one's own scholarly mentors is strictly forbidden.)

Whatever shenanigans Cronus was up to, he never forgot that a son of his was fated to replace him, and with the hard-headed nuttiness typical of the gods he tried to outwit the Fates. As each of Rhea's children, Hestia, Demeter, Hera, Hades, and the rest were born, he swallowed them. Rhea reacted to this mistreatment of her offspring quite as angrily as had Gaia. When she was about to bear Zeus, she begged for the help of her parents Earth and Heaven in stopping Cronus' infanticide. They directed her to the land of Crete, where Gaia received the babe to be brought up on Mount Aegeum. Rhea gave Cronus a stone wrapped in a baby blanket, which he swallowed with no comment. This indicates that he had very little discernment or taste, but a marvelous digestive system. When Zeus was grown and powerful, Rhea provided Cronus with an emetic, and his children sprang forth unharmed (which gives us second thoughts about that digestive system). Thus began the War of the Gods, with Altas leading the Titans and Zeus, aided by Prometheus, leading the opposition. (*Theogony, ll. 617-885*). The Greeks remembered Cronus kindly, and he had some of the smaller, older temples and a feast day or two connected with the harvest, but his glory days were largely past.

1. B. Roman/Saturn

Saturn was an ancient Italian deity. He was identified with Cronos, and like Cronus he was king of the gods before Jupiter and his brothers, Neptune and Pluto, staged a coup and overthrew their father. After his dethronement by Jupiter Saturn fled to Italy, where he reigned during what was called the Golden Age, a time of peace and prosperity that the cynical associated with the time before Jupiter ordered the creation of woman. The memory of his Golden Age was celebrated every year with the festival of Saturnalia, which started on December 17 and ran for 7 days. Then all public business was suspended, declarations of war and criminal executions were postponed, friends made presents to one another, and the slaves were indulged with great liberties. A feast was given the slaves during which they sat at table, while their masters served them, to show not only the natural equality of men, but also that all things belonged equally to all in the reign of Saturn (which was far enough into the dim past that the haves need not fear the have-nots would get any undesirable ideas).

Rhea, Mother of the Gods
"daughter of earth and sky, whose chariot is drawn by fierce lions"
Orphic Hymn to Rhea

2. Rhea/ Roman Ops

Rhea seems to have spent an inordinate amount of time beating on a brass drum when she was not bearing future Olympians, rescuing and rehabilitating rascally young gods such as Dionysus, trying unsuccessfully to control Zeus, or catching Cronus in misdeeds. The plane tree represented her green hand. Along with Metis, she was spared punishment at the end of the war of the gods. (Perhaps even Zeus felt he had put these two through quite enough). In time, she became confused with her mother Gaia, with the Phrygian goddess Cybele, and with other personifications of Mother Earth.

3. Iapetus

Iapetus was one of those poor souls destined to be completely overshadowed by his sons, the great Prometheus and the mighty Atlas. At least, according to the psychiatrists, that is less damaging to the ego than being overshadowed by one's father. Iapetus' wife the "neat-ankled maid Clymene," (*The Theogony, l. 507*) bore him these two and also poor bumbling Epimetheus, as well as Menoetius whom Zeus sent to Erebus with a thunderbolt because of his "mad presumption and exceeding pride." (*The Theogony, l. 522*)

4. Oceanus

Oceanus was the god of the river Ocean, which encircled the world; some say he and his wife Tethys were the origin of all living things. He sometimes got a bit playful: when Heracles was sailing on the Mediterranean in the golden water lily goblet of the predecessor of Apollo, the sun god Helios (who evidently had very peculiar ideas about sailing craft), Oceanus made it pitch unmercifully. Heracles, never much for being the butt of jokes, threatened him angrily with an arrow. Exactly what harm this could have done to the river Ocean seems a bit hazy, but he calmed the waves.

5. Tethys

Tethys, the wife of Ocean, was kept busy being mother of his many children. One of the more outstanding of their many daughters was the dread Nemesis, who sneaked up behind wrong-doers and saw that they got their come-uppance (no doubt she was one of the busiest of all the immortals). Another was Dione, who shared the oracle at Dodona with Zeus and in some versions of the myths is the mother of Aphrodite/Venus.

6. Atlas

Iapetus' son Atlas was the war leader of the Titans against the Olympians, and paid the high price of losing. He was condemned to bear the sky (or in some stories the world) on his shoulders. Because of some inhospitality,

Perseus turned him into a mountain (or a whole mountain range). He became father of the Hesperides and the Pleiades, evidently before either of the above-listed uncomfortable developments.

7. Prometheus

The very name Prometheus means Forethought. As the wisest of the Titans, he correctly divined the winning side in the war of the gods and joined Zeus/Jupiter. When the war was over Zeus was well pleased with Prometheus (a state of affairs that would not last long), and according to some stories commissioned him and his bubble-headed brother Epimetheus to give living creatures to the beautiful earth now under his control. Epimetheus had a wonderful time creating animals and giving them strength and swiftness and cunning, wings and claws and shells, fur and feathers. Meanwhile Prometheus labored on the production of a man-creature, more noble, (or at least better-looking, as Prometheus modeled him after himself), than any beast. But when he had finished his creation, he discovered that Epimetheus had given all the good protective gifts, such as those mentioned above, to the animals. Therefore Prometheus did the best he could to shield man. When men and Zeus disputed over the division of animal offerings, Prometheus dressed up the inedible bones in rich fat and concealed the edible parts in a mangy hide. Zeus, invited to choose, chose the better-looking pile and found himself hoodwinked -- ever after men would keep the best parts for themselves. While Zeus was glowering over this, Prometheus went to Heaven and brought down fire in hollow fennel stalk and gave it to mankind so that he might warm himself, cook his food, and have light and protection against the animals.

At this point Zeus had the first (but unfortunately not the last) Olympian rage. Hesiod says that he was stung in spirit. However that may have been, he was mad as a hornet. He vowed revenge on Prometheus, but he would devise something really brilliant a little later on for that – an imaginative vengeance that would turn Prometheus into the symbol of unbreakable spirit under unjust torture. But first Zeus turned his mind to man and how best to undo him. Epimetheus looked like a likely place to start.

8. Epimetheus

The name of this heedless brother of Prometheus means Afterthought, and he lived up to his title with enthusiasm. He had complicated Prometheus' work producing man and now promptly proceeded to forget

Prometheus' directive that he never accept a gift from Zeus. Perhaps that was understandable, considering the gift in question. At this point mankind was exactly that – man. The age was Golden, and the living was easy. It was always Spring, the flowers were always blooming, the fish biting, and the deer standing around waiting to be shot. However, companionship of the gentle and aesthetic sort was definitely lacking. Zeus set out, in a far from helpful spirit, to correct this lack. The poet Hesiod, who shows an anti-feminine spirit likely to bring fainting spells to the disciples of political correctness, says that Hephaestus/Vulcan, following Zeus's directions, made an evil thing out of earth and gave it the appearance of a shy maiden. This beautiful evil, he thunders, was to be the price paid for the gift of fire. The beauty of her silvery clothing, embroidered veil, and head-garlands of flowers, all provided by Athena/Minerva, was augmented by her bright eyes and the happy expression brought on by her delight in her fine clothes. Gods and men were astounded at the sight of her, and their awe was only increased by her crown, which Athena/Minerva placed last of all upon her head. This incredible specimen of Hephaestus/Vulcan's art was not only beautifully wrought in intricate gold work, but was decorated with creatures of the land and sea rearing up and speaking like living beings with voices. Needless to say, Pandora, whose name means gifts of all, stunned all beholders.

Hesiod, still striving for the title of Misogynist of the Year, if not of All Time, says that from her came the deadly race of women, who have the nature to do mischief. Getting a bit mixed up in his biology, he compares them to drones in a bee-hive, and indicates that drones stay at home and eat what others prepare and do nothing to earn their keep. (Delicacy forbids us to delineate in this treatise exactly how drone bees do earn their keep, which in any case is not precisely what women do). With a cheery outlook worthy of the pessimistic philosopher Schopenhauer, he then complains that whoever simply avoids women encounters a second evil, as he has no offspring to tend him in his declining years, and after his death his relatives will get all his possessions. And even if the hapless male manages to find a good wife (which he seems to consider highly unlikely) he may rear mischievous children who will be an everlasting grief to him. (*Theogony*, l. 561-613)

The gods, Hesiod regrets to tell us, set Pandora down in a flowery meadow. Prometheus came by, took one look, and declared that she looked like trouble with a capital T. Epimetheus, sauntering by a bit later, was charmed and took her home with him.

Now mythologists agree that Pandora brought great grief to mankind by opening something she shouldn't have opened. Some say it was a box, but the oldest texts seem to indicate a jar. Some say Zeus gave it to her to bring along when she was deposited in the meadow; others say it was already in the residence of Prometheus and Epimetheus when she arrived. Everybody agrees that it contained all the plagues and ills that so easily lay waste mankind, and that Prometheus, and perhaps Zeus/Jupiter, gave Pandora strict instructions not to open it, but, in the negligent (and arrogant) manner of males, didn't bother to tell her why. One morning after Prometheus and Epimetheus had gone out hunting, or fishing, or just messing about, Pandora cleaned up the residence, washed the dishes, and found nothing else to do but wonder what was in that jar. She recalled her instructions: Zeus had told her not to open it; Epimetheus had begged her not to open it; Prometheus had indicated he might break her neck if she opened it. But, surely, she reasoned, it wouldn't hurt to take a tiny peek. Once the lid was ajar, however, all those unpleasant things, furiously resenting their incarceration, flew out and started wreaking havoc on the earth. They are still wreaking, and poor curious Pandora and all succeeding females get the blame.

Chapter III - Olympians and/or Dii Consentes

Now we must take a look at the histories, as carefully edited by the conquering invaders, of the best-known and most powerful platoon of Greek gods, those who lived in Thessaly on Olympus, the highest mountain in Greece. For the sake of order (which never fares well when confronted with mythology), let us try to line up the legendary Twelve Great Olympians. (Not that we can do this without ruffling a few feathers. Some say that Pluto/Hades and even Poseidon do not truly belong to Olympus, as they are not sky gods. Others get huffy about the rights of Demeter or Dionysus. To complicate matters that need no complication, according to the Roman poet Ennius, who lived in the 3rd century BC, the group of twelve Gods especially honored by the Romans, called the Dii Consentes, were Jupiter, Juno, Minerva, Vesta, Ceres, Diana, Venus, Mars, Mercury, Neptune, Vulcan, and Apollo. Evidently Ceres, the grain goddess, the counterpart of Greek Demeter, made their Great Gods list in place of Pluto/Hades. To help frustrated students avoid terminal high blood pressure, however, let us give the traditional line-up and take up the complications later. Organizing the Olympians, a task which we are about to undertake, bears a close resemblance to organizing a basket of puppies, but here goes. First, we shall take a brief overview, and then discuss some of the gossipy details for each.

Twelve Olympians

1. Zeus/Jupiter - He dethroned his father Cronus/Saturn and took his place as Lord of Sky and Earth and Superintendent of the Universe. His bird was the eagle; his tree the oak; his chief oracle was located at Dodona.

2. Hera/Juno - She was the wife and sister of Zeus/Jupiter, Queen of Sky and Earth and the protectress of marriage. Her animal was the cow; her bird was the peacock.

3. Poseidon/Neptune - This brother of Jupiter was god of the sea. His animal was the horse. His wife was Amphitrite, one of Ocean's granddaughters.

4. Pluto/Hades- This dreaded figure was ruler of the lower world (the dead). His stolen bride was Persephone/Proserpina.

5. Hestia/Vesta - The quiet and chaste goddess of fireplace was the sister of Zeus/Jupiter. Every meal included a sacrifice to her as guardian of the home. Cities had a public fire of Hestia/Vesta.

6. Pallas Athena/Minerva - The daughter of Zeus alone, as she sprang from his head, she was goddess of wisdom and protectress of civilized life. Her city was Athens; her tree, the olive; her bird, the owl.

7. Phoebus Apollo- He was the son of Jupiter and Leto (Latona) and twin brother of Artemis/Diana. He was god of medicine, truth, music, and the sun. His tree was the laurel; his bird, the crow; his fish, the dolphin. As he was god of truth, his oracle at Delphi was very important.

8. Artemis/Diana- She began as the twin sister of Apollo, but later became a three-fold deity: the goddess of hunting (Artemis), of witches (Hecate), and of the moon (Selene). Her tree was the cypress and her animal was the deer, though all animals were under her protection.

9. Aphrodite/Venus - The powerful goddess of love and beauty sprang from the sea. (In some tales, she was the daughter of Zeus and Dione). Her bird was the dove; her tree, the myrtle.

10. Ares/Mars - This fearful son of Zeus/Jupiter and Hera/Juno was the god of war. Thus, his bird was the vulture; his animal was the dog or wolf.

11. Hermes/Mercury - This swift, wing-footed god was the son of Zeus/Jupiter and Maia. He was the god of speed, trade, and thieves, as well as messenger of the gods.

12. Hephaestus/Vulcan - The only ugly god on Mt. Olympus was son of Hera/Juno. He was god of fire and blacksmith of Olympus. His wife was Aphrodite/Venus.

The above listed are the Twelve Great Olympians. Readers of a pessimistic nature have probably already suspected that there are others, and indeed, there are. At a later time we will try to bring them in as painlessly as possible. For the present, the Big Twelve are more than enough to deal with.

1. A. Zeus, King of Gods and Father of Men

Now to settle down to the facts (using the term loosely) concerning the aforesaid Big Twelve. When one thinks of Olympians, Zeus naturally springs to mind. This tome has already mentioned that, when full-grown after being reared in Crete, Zeus marshaled his newly liberated brothers and sisters for a full-scale war on his father Cronus. (Honoring one's parents is not always stressed in classical mythology. Perhaps, though, that is understandable, considering the traumatic adolescent years of Cronus' offspring.) With the single exception of the wise Prometheus, who sided with Zeus, the Titans fought on the side of Cronus, so Zeus, hoping to even the score a bit, released all those decidedly unpleasant offspring of Gaia whom Ouranus had imprisoned under the earth. Hesiod says that in gratitude to him for his kindness (or in a furious desire to get even with Ouranus, Cronus, and anyone else who got in their way), they gave him thunder and the glowing thunderbolt and lightening, which Mother Earth had kept hidden heretofore. They then employed all their resources, such as their fifty heads and hundred hands, in the service of their nephew Zeus. In the forefront of the battle Cottus, Briareos, and Gyes raised and launched three hundred rocks, while Zeus let loose the afore-mentioned thunder and lightening. It is not surprising that the Titans suffered a resounding defeat.

Zeus soon proved to be master of many arts, one of which was devising punishments for those who displeased him. Altas was condemned to bear the sky on his shoulders as his reward for leading the losing side, and other Titans were awarded varying penalties. Most found themselves down in Tartarus (a singularly unprepossessing portion of the Underworld which we shall explore later) loaded down with chains. (One of the disadvantages of a War Between the Gods is that gods are typically impossible to kill, and the winner finds himself saddled with a large troop of disgruntled POWs). We have already mentioned that it did not take Prometheus long to dissipate the good-will Zeus had felt for him while the war was being waged. For his part in giving man a foot-hold on survival, Zeus had Prometheus chained to a rock and sent an eagle (which was his special bird) to eat his immortal liver by day; by night the liver grew as much again as the bird had devoured in the day. (The ancients believed that the liver, rather than the heart, was the seat of all emotion. One shudders to think what this concept could do to the Valentine business). The appalling liver-devouring process went on for thirty thousand years, until Heracles slew the bird. Zeus was still miffed, but he wanted his son Heracles to have credit for this great deed, so he kept quiet.

Having settled the Titan question, Zeus and his two brothers, Poseidon and Pluto, drew lots for their realms. To Poseidon fell the sea, and to Pluto the underworld. Zeus, keeping fast hold on those thunderbolts, became Lord of the Sky and general Superintendent of the Universe. He regulated the heavenly bodies, made laws, enforced oaths and pronounced oracles at Dodona in Epirus. (However, his son Apollo, the god of truth, soon drew more business in this last respect and developed a much more impressive shrine). Beside the marble splendor of Apollo's Delphi, Zeus's oracle at Dodona resembled a Spartan war camp. Homer said that the priests there had no buildings and slept on the ground; their business was to tend an ancient grove of very special sacred oaks. The rustling of the oak leaves, carefully interpreted by these priests, foretold the future. Evidently, these trees' fortune-telling powers were not confined to their leaves; when Jason and the Argonauts set sail, the ship Argo had the gift of prophecy because it was made of oak wood from Dodona. (In pre-Hellenic times this unpretentious but powerful place had belonged to the Earth Mother, who the inscriptions indicate was known here as Dione. When we get to the story of Aphrodite, we will find an interesting sidelight on this mythological tidbit.)

We have seen that Zeus took very decisive action in the case of Prometheus and also of mankind. As a result, when he set up shop as Commander-in-Chief no one was inclined to quibble about his orders.

Zeus now set out to rear his own family. Here matters get rather sticky, as those afore-mentioned Indo-European (or Hellenic, or whatever) invaders found a land (or several lands, really) populated by peoples already developing city-states (most of which were little villages with big ideas) and paying tribute to one of the other of a plethora of female deities. In order to proclaim sovereignty over each area, the Hellenes solemnly announced that Zeus was the husband and/or overlord of each supreme female deity. Thus Hesiod lists a gaggle of wives, starting with Metis, the powerful goddess of wisdom, whom Zeus imprisoned in his belly so that he might not lose control of her offspring, Athena. Athena, as we have mentioned, was said to be born from Zeus' head, wearing armor yet. That took care of any nonsense about matriarchal superiority and set a new standard for what dramatists call "the willing suspension of disbelief," which is a *sine qua non* of mythology study.

Wife number two according to Hesiod was Themis, who bore to Zeus the Horae (Hours), and Eunomia (Order), Dike (Justice), and Eirene

(Peace), as well as the dreadful Moerae or Fates -- Clotho, Lachesis, and Atropos. (As the decrees of the Fates are absolute and cannot be gainsaid even by Zeus himself, this story seems incongruous. But that in no way renders it unique in the annals of mythology.)

Next came Eurynome, the daughter of Ocean, mother of the Graces, Aglaea, and Euphrosyne, and Thaleia, whose glance, Hesiod informs us, is beautiful beneath their brows. (That is comforting, as this is by far the best place for a glance, beautiful or not, to be located.)

Next on the program was Demeter/Ceres, the grain goddess, mother of Persephone/Proserpina whom Pluto carried off in a zesty little adventure we shall chronicle later.

Zeus' next listed wife was Mnemosyne or Memory, with whom he lay nine nights. The results of this extended rendezvous were the nine Muses[2].

Leto was not the first but certainly one of the most influential of Zeus' wives, as her children were Apollo the sun god and Artemis, goddess of the moon and of hunting. As we shall see, these powerful deities took a dim view of anyone's speaking slightingly of their mother and dealt quite decisively with such *lese majeste*.

Last in his catalogue of Zeus' temporary **inamoratae** Hesiod lists Semele, daughter of Cadmus, who bore Dionysus god of wine. (*Theogony ll. 900-942*) Evidently, Hera was already at this time the wife of Zeus. As Semele drew near the time to deliver her child, after Zeus had rashly sworn by the infernal river Styx that he would do what she asked, Hera inspired Semele to ask to see him in his full glory. Zeus begged her to choose another boon, for he knew no mortal could see him so and live. But she was adamant, and he had sworn the unbreakable oath. When he came before her in full regalia, she was burned to death in the blinding fiery light. Zeus, who had seen all along how this dismal affair would end, snatched her baby from her and sewed it into his side until it was ready to be born. (This bizarre incident led to worshippers addressing Dionysus and "the insewn.") Later Dionysus braved the World of the Dead to retrieve his mother, and Hesiod says that after this they were both gods.

Of course, all along we have been building up to Hera, Zeus' eternal wife and sparring partner. She bore him not only Hebe the cup-bearer but also Ares, the powerful if not scholarly god of war. According to Hesiod, she was angry with Zeus (perhaps over this gaggle of wives) and bore Hephaestus, the god of fire, on her own without his help. Sometime during all these soap opera developments Maia, the daughter of Atlas, bore to Zeus Hermes, the messenger god concerned with merchants, speed and trade.

Zeus may have been a philandering husband who occasionally wriggled a bit to avoid his wife's wrath (and as we move along we will see abundant proof of this), but that lamentable fact in no way diminished his awesome majesty or his power. When Thetis, the lovely sea-nymph, who was mother of the great Greek warrior Achilles, was beseeching him to give let the Trojans win because the Greeks had mistreated her son, Homer says that, after quibbling a bit about Hera's probable reaction and telling Thetis to play least in sight because of it, Zeus intoned solemnly, "After consideration, I shall do as you wish. See, I incline my head so you may believe me. This is the most solemn oath that I can give to any god. I never recall my word, or deceive, or fail to do what I say, when I have nodded my head." (This leads us to wonder what happened when he spoke without the nod). He then lowered his glowing countenance, and the ambrosial locks swayed on his immortal head, til vast Olympus reeled. (Homer, *Iliad I, 520-526*) No doubt the snowy peaks rang with the shouts of deities large and small, "Hit the deck! Zeus the Father is nodding again."

•

1. B. Roman Jupiter

Before we go into Jupiter's story, we need to take a peek at his Roman background, which is somewhat different from that of Zeus. At the founding of Rome, the gods were *'numina'*, divine manifestations, faceless, formless, but very powerful. The idea of gods in human form came later, with the influence from Etruscans (a highly developed and exceedingly warlike people who were neighbors of Rome to the north) and Greeks. For the Romans, everything in Nature was inhabited by *numina*, which manifested the divine will by means of natural phenomena that the pious Roman constantly sought to interpret. Thus, great attention was paid to omens and portents in every aspect of Roman daily life. The priestly college of augurs interpreted every aspect of the flights of birds, as they believed that the birds were messengers of Jupiter whose movements showed his decrees. Cicero speaks of birds as Jupiter's messengers and of the augurs, of whose college he was a member, as the interpreters of Jupiter Optimus Maximus (*De Legibus II, 8*)

As mentioned before, the Poet Ennius in the 3rd Century BCE lists as most honored by the Romans a group of twelve Gods called Dii Consentes: Iuppiter, Iuno, Minerva, Vesta, Ceres, Diana, Venus, Mars, Mercurius, Neptunus, Volcanus, and Apollo. Their gilt statues stood in the Forum, later apparently in the Porticus Deorum Consentium. They were probably the twelve worshipped in 217 BCE at a *lectisternium*, which tongue-twisting term means a banquet of the gods at which the statues of the gods were put upon cushions and were offered meals. Although the Etruscans also worshipped a main pantheon of twelve Gods, the Dii Consentes were not identified with Etruscan deities but rather with the Greek Olympian Gods (though obviously the original character of the Roman Gods was different from the Greek). The twelve Dii Consentes were lead by the first three, Jupiter, Juno, and Minerva. These form the Capitoline Triad whose rites were conducted in the Capitoleum Vetus on the Capitoline Hill.

All these differences notwithstanding Jupiter, or Jove Pater, in classical times corresponded in many aspects to Zeus. (Rome's chief god had a collection of names even more confusing than most, as the Romans called him Jove, then added pater, or father, when addressing him or speaking of him as a subject. This was contracted to Juppiter (Jupiter). In all other constructions he is Jove. (Confused persons thus swear by Jupiter, or by Jove, possibly not pausing to consider that this is the same thing. Of course, in the heat of self-expression they probably don't care). Whatever one called him, this son of Saturn and brother of Juno (who was also his wife) was the supreme god of the Roman pantheon. Like Zeus he wielded the lightning bolt, and the eagle was both his symbol and his messenger. In addition to being the ruler of the sky, he was also the protector of the state and its laws. Since added to the double or triple names with which they were saddled, Roman deities usually got extra names for their duties, in his protector role he was Jupiter Optimus Maximus (Best and Greatest). His other titles include Caelestis (heavenly), Lucetius (of the light), Tonans (thunderer), and Fulgurator (of the lightning). As Jupiter Victor he led the Roman army to victory, and in his spare time was the protector of the Latin League (an ancient confederation of Italian city-states basically independent but bound together by the necessity of defending themselves against their various enemies).

He shared a great temple on the Capitoline [3] Hill with Juno and Minerva, but he was the most prominent of the three. Before the eyebrow-raising stories about Zeus were added to his biography, he was a very majestic, extremely powerful, and slightly dull father figure.

2. A. Hera, Queen of the Gods

We have already seen that Hera seems to come late on Zeus' list of wives, but she became the permanent and supreme one in a hurry. Perhaps this is because she had long been patroness of some cities that threw their weight around, and had a good bit of it to throw. Zeus wooed her soon after the successful completion of the war of the gods, but she was not impressed. He finally won her over by adopting the guise of a bedraggled cuckoo (a pose that, if looks and behavior are any indications, other lovers through the ages have adopted from time to time). Hera made the mistake of warming this pathetic creature in her bosom. He took shameless advantage of her pity, and she soon found herself chief exhibit at a wedding. (Wooing among the gods was generally a rough and tumble sport, woefully short on candy and flowers.) At least she got some outstanding wedding gifts, including a tree bearing golden apples, gift of Gaia, which the Hesperides guarded for her.

Hera was the protectress of marriage, which in her personal case took a good deal of protecting. Zeus, not limiting his conquests to the immortals, also indulged some earthly amours. He fell in love with a princess named Io, daughter of King Inachus, and troubled her dreams until at last she agreed to meet him. Taking precaution against the anger of Hera, which he had but too much cause to want to circumvent, Zeus wrapped himself and Io in a dark cloud. Hera noticed this little blip on the weather screen and dived down from Mount Olympus to check things out. Zeus, who was more than half expecting such a visit, turned Io into a beautiful white heifer which he blithely explained to his wife had just sprung from the earth. (Ovid mentions that lovers swearing false oaths should always swear by Zeus, who is in no position to cast stones). "How lovely," she cooed. "Make me a present of it." Before Zeus could think of an excuse (which probably wouldn't have been of the least use anyway), Hera had driven poor Io away and delivered her into the care of Argus. He was not one of those giants who had one hundred heads or one hundred hands, but, from Hera's point of view, he had a much more useful attribute -- one hundred eyes, of which only two slept at a time. Zeus had no chance to change Io back, thanks to Argus' zeal.

Although gods are not much given to self-blame, Zeus could not escape the feeling that Io's plight could possibly be his fault. He sent his son Hermes to lull Argus to sleep and free Io. After a number of long (and evidently incredibly dull) stories, all Argus' eyes closed in sleep, and Hermes slew him. Hera grieved for Argus, and set his hundred eyes in the tail of the peacock, which became her bird. She then sent a gadfly to torment poor bovine Io and drive her from land to land. (During her wanderings, a number of geographical features were named for her, such as the Ionian Sea and the Bosporus [Cow-ford]. Thoughtful people doubt, however, that she received much comfort from this.) Finally her torments so affected Zeus that he made full confession to Hera and promised never to have dealings with Io again if Hera would restore her to her proper form. This Hera did, and Io went gratefully back to her homeland. Zeus had learned a valuable lesson. Unfortunately, this lesson was not: "Don't cheat on your wife," but rather "Don't cheat on your wife in your own form."

The next object of Zeus' affection (at least from a geographical point of view) was Europa, who according to Hesiod was one of the many nymphs who were daughters of Oceanus. Hera was evidently busy otherwise; the tryst seems to have brought no retribution on this maiden. Europa had a strange dream early one morning about two females, one named Asia and one nameless, each claiming ownership of her. Understandably, the girl found sleep under these conditions trying, if not impossible. She roused her unfortunate ladies-in-waiting out of their beauty sleep for a bit of early flower gathering. While Zeus was sitting on a cloud watching the girls flitting about gathering posies, Venus (or more likely her mischievous son Eros/Amor/ Cupid) zapped Zeus with a golden arrow. For the uninitiated, that meant that he would fall in love with the next female he saw. As he was looking at Europa, this didn't take long. Remembering all too clearly what had happened last time, he turned himself into a beautiful chestnut-colored bull. In every way an unusual example of the bovine species, he had a silver circle on his brow and horns like a crescent moon. Further departing from qualities generally seen in bulls, he had a musical low and a heavenly fragrance. After shrieking a bit, the girls drew near this amazing creature who stood very still and seemed very gentle. He lay down at Europa's feet and lowed enticingly. She sat down on his back, only to be carried to the sea, which was, fortunately or unfortunately, nearby. Europa was hardly a great intellectual, but, as the bull moved not into, but over the waters, and all sorts of water gods, singing romantic melodies, accompanied them, she decided there was something a bit unusual about this bull. When she questioned him, he admitted that he was Zeus himself, and was taking her to Crete, where she would bear him outstanding sons. (No doubt, he said this softly, keeping a weather eye out for Hera). Two of her sons, Minos and Rhadamanthus, were outstanding indeed, as after death they became judges of the dead in Hades because they had shown themselves pillars of justice on earth. It has probably occurred to our clever readers by this time that the nameless lady contending with Asia for the maiden was the continent of Europe.

But as this is supposed to be a section devoted to Hera, let us get back to the amours she did discover. Zeus, still observing precautions, visited

Alcmena, the wife of Amphitryon, in the guise of her husband. This evidently worked splendidly until Zeus, in a moment of hare-brained euphoria, boasted that a son soon to be born to him who would be High King of the mighty house of Perseus. Hera, (who never seemed to miss these little tidbits) hindered Alcmena's delivery so that another queen would bear her son first, making him heir to the high kingship. Alcmena bore two sons, Iphicles to Amphitryon and the great Heracles to Zeus. Hera, still in a far from friendly mood, made the first of her many plans for enlivening Heracles' life. She sent two giant serpents into the cradle of Heracles and Iphicles when they were not yet one year old. Hearing the screams of Iphicles, Alcmena ran into the nursery to find Heracles laughing and holding a strangled snake in each hand. In no way discouraged, Hera set out to torment Heracles with the same thorough nastiness she would show in dealing with the Trojans after the Trojan War.

Another unfortunate maiden who caught Zeus' wandering eye was the princess Callisto. Zeus saw her hunting in the train of Artemis (who had a whole regiment of beautiful maidens sworn to chastity and devoted to such masculine pursuits). Like Artemis herself, these maidens remained virgins, but Zeus, still in the business of assuming disguises, came near Callisto in the form of Artemis herself and overpowered her. When Artemis (who had the usual divine attributes of taking offense at everything and never listening to excuses) discovered that Callisto was pregnant, the princess was banished and left to bear her child alone. When the child was born, Hera changed Callisto into a bear, and she wandered the forest watching her son Arcas grow up from afar. Hera, still out for blood, brought young Arcas, now a fine hunter, face to face with Callisto. Before he could spear the bear Zeus placed Callisto in the sky as the constellation Ursa Major, or "great bear," and then took Arcas and placed him in the sky near his mother as Ursa Minor, the "little bear." Hera, determined to have the last say in the matter, went to her nurse, Tethys, the wife of Oceanus, and beseeched her to punish Callisto and Arcas. Tethys decided to deprive the pair of water, and so the great bear and the little bear are cursed to circle in the skies, never to dip below the horizon for a refreshing bath or a cool drink (neither of which seems a great deprivation for a collection of stars). Thus the ancients explained why the two constellations are circumpolar, visible all year round.

In her spare time, Hera led a revolt of the Olympians against Zeus. The Olympian family was proving as obstreperous as any offspring in a modern drama, and had a growing resentment of Father Zeus' extremely arbitrary ways. Only Hestia failed to join in Hera's ill-fated uprising, which ended with the queen of the gods suspended in the sky by golden chains until all the other gods promised never again to revolt against Zeus. All reluctantly swore (though evidently some crossed their fingers). All but Apollo and Poseidon (who had sided with Hera even after losing a contest with her for Chief Divinity of Argos) were pardoned without punishment; these two were sent as bond-servants to King Laomedon, for whom they built the city of Troy. After this misadventure Hera confined her attempts to control or influence Zeus to nagging and raging, which had some effect, and winning him over by her beauty, a device which, as Homer makes clear in *Iliad 14*, worked quite well when she took the time and patience to use it.

All this jealous rage and spousal war in no way diminished Hera's majesty, however. An anonymous Greek poet in one of the ancient Homeric Hymns (which actually have nothing to do with Homer) says, "I sing of Hera of the golden throne, immortal queen whom Rhea bore, radiant in beauty, sister and wife of loud-thundering Zeus; she is the illustrious one whom all the blessed ones throughout high Olympus hold in awe and honor, just as they do Zeus who delights in this lightning and thunder." (*Homeric Hymn Number 12, To Hera*). Pausanias credits the legendary poet Olen, said to have been the first priest of Apollo, with a hymn to Hera (whether or not it was Number 12 only Olympus knows). Her many temples and holy places were filled with suppliants asking her favor and keeping a wary eye out for any signs of her displeasure.

2. B. Roman Juno

Juno was an imposing and powerful figure, guardian and special counselor of the Roman state and queen of the gods. She was protector of the Roman people and especially women, being the goddess of marriage, fertility and all aspects of pregnancy and childbirth. Like Jupiter, she had a wealth of titles. As the matron goddess of Rome and the Roman Empire, she was called Regina ("queen"). She was worshiped as Juno Capitolina as part of the Capitoline Triad, in conjunction with Jupiter and Minerva, at the temple on the Capitoline Hill in Rome. From her title "Juno Moneta" comes the modern word "money," as the Roman mint was built close to her temple on the Arx, one of the two prongs of the Capitoline hill. (Where she got the title Moneta is more problematic. She had that name long before the first coin was struck. Some say it comes from "mons" or mountain, some from "monere" to warn, perhaps because her sacred geese warned the Romans when the Gauls tried to take the Capitolium in 390 BC.[4]

The cynical said that one of her functions was to warn those considering marriage.) Juno Sospita (Savior), who had her own festival on February 1st, was the patron goddess of the state, and her temple for this function was in the Forum Holitorium in Rome. As Juno Curitis or Juno Quiritis, the protector of spearmen, she had a temple on the Campus Martius. She was the only deity to be worshipped by all 30 **curiae**, the Roman military and administrative units introduced by Romulus.

By the second century BCE, Juno Lucina was associated with light (lux) and childbirth. When a child was born, it was said to have been "brought to light." With her daughter Ilithyia, Juno aided women in childbirth, which has always been a somewhat perilous undertaking. Women worshipping Juno Lucina had to untie knots and unbraid their hair lest these entanglements symbolically block delivery of a child. Of the many forms of her seen on coins, the most common show her as Juno Lucina, with a child in her arms and two more at her feet, or Juno Regina, in which case she is adorned with the scepter and veil, and accompanied by a peacock.

In many ways she seems more truly divine than Hera. She was the great Protectress, watching over marriage and married women and honoring their love. She so pitied Alcyone when her husband Ceyx died at sea that she turned the pair of them into birds so they could be together. (Ovid, *Metamorphoses, book XI*) However, according to Vergil (who may have been influenced by Homer's and other Greeks' opinion of Hera) she never forgot a slight, real or fancied. He makes her stubborn demand for the annihilation of the Trojans a major driving force in the *Aeneid*.

3. A. Poseidon, God of the Sea

Son of Cronos and Rhea, brother of Zeus, Hades, Hestia, Demeter and Hera, Poseidon was one of the older Olympians, and he answered to no one except Zeus. (Sometimes he forgot to answer even to him. He not only aided Hera in her revolt, but also went down to the battlefield at Troy and took a hand in matters although Zeus had forbidden such activity [*Iliad 15*]). His kingdom was the vast sea, where he lived on the ocean floor in a palace made of coral and gems and populated his watery realm with creatures of his own design. He liked to surprise the pretty little nymphs with monsters; he concocted the octopus, the blowfish, and the seapolyp just to hear them squeal. People who lived near the sea and inlanders as well (as his floods reached far into the countryside) went to great lengths to keep him happy. In the hope of pleasing him, the Greeks sometimes drowned sacrificial horses in his honor (one of many evidences that the ancient world stood in crying need of an SPCA). Poseidon's sea provided a fine income for sailors, and when in a good mood, he not only supplied a calm sea but also created new lands in the water. He could turn nasty in an instant, however, producing terrible storms that had drastic effects on ships and those in them (as well as on the financial solvency of those who invested in them). In addition to this, Homer called him the earth shaker, probably because when moody or depressed he would shake both earth and sea with his trident and cause earthquakes and odd springs of water on land in addition to creating the afore mentioned storms at sea. He pounded land and water in anger, in pleasure, or just for the fun of it, riding the waves in a chariot drawn by dolphins, horses, or, (contribution of the logical) sea horses. It is obvious why Poseidon was called the god of earthquakes, and, for reasons we shall now explore, he was also the god of horses.

Longing to be the patron deity of an outstanding city or two like the other gods, Poseidon got into various squabbles with the other divinities while trying to achieve this goal. According to some myths he came to Athens where, with a blow of his trident on the Acropolis, he produced a sea or perhaps just the well of sea-water. Pallas Athena also laid claim to this high city, and the Athenians, who were never slow to take advantage of a promising situation, devised a competition between her and Poseidon. The giver of the best gift would be their chief divinity and their city would carry his or her name. Athena created the olive tree, and won, but in the heat of competition Poseidon, not settling for that salty spring, created the horse and changed the shape of history. (For those less than impressed with the Athenians' choice of beneficial gifts, we mention that the olive tree gave fruit, oil for cooking and preservation of food as well as hair dressing and lamp fuel, wood for many purposes, and leaves used for medicine).

Poseidon resembled his brother Zeus in amorous eagerness. He had many love affairs and fathered numerous children, among whom the Cyclops Polyphemus, the hero Bellerophon, and even the winged horse Pegasus are sometimes placed. (Since this particular Pegasus myth states that the horse's mother was the Gorgon Medusa, [5] Poseidon must have been a far from faint-hearted lover.) When he decided to marry the Oceanid Amphitrite, she, wishing to remain a virgin, fled to Mount Altas. Poseidon then sent many of his creatures to look for her. A certain dolphin found her, persuaded her to marry Poseidon, and took charge of the wedding himself. After this triple duty as detective, advocate, and bridal consultant, it is small wonder that Poseidon made the dolphin into a constellation of stars in the sky.

Poseidon also had a fair-sized streak of divine vengefulness. He might have forgiven the Greek hero Odysseus for blinding his son, the Cyclops Polyphemus, who after all was trying to eat Odysseus and all his men, if only Odysseus had not been one of those vaunting Greek heroes who could never keep his mouth closed. After he had blinded Polyphemus and was sailing away from the island of Sicily, he taunted Polyphemus, saying that not even his father Poseidon could restore the sight that he, the great Odysseus, had taken away. This was not very wise of him, since he was venturing forth on Poseidon's sea, as his weary followers tried to warn him. But Odysseus had a full measure of the foolhardy daring that characterizes so many heroes, so he went right on taunting Polyphemus. Poseidon would happily have drowned him except for the fact that those know-it-all Fates had decreed that Odysseus would return to his kingdom of Ithaca. He did get there, but Poseidon saw to it that he arrived alone, beggared, late, and in a borrowed ship, only to find his house full of enemies.

When not stirring up storms, avenging insults, or pursuing maidens, Poseidon was quite a construction engineer. Not only did his taking the wrong side of squabbles lead to his building a great part of Troy, but he also constructed the brazen fence that surrounds Tartarus and its gates of bronze, behind which the Titans were confined.

3. B. Roman Neptune, God of Waters

Neptune was originally simply the god of all waters for Romans, as well as Neptune Equester, creator of the horse. In the early days they had as little to do with the sea as possible, but as their history advanced they not only fell under Greek influence but also acquired some extra-peninsular enemies. As they felt the need of divine protection when dealing with the always moody Mediterranean, Neptune was therefore promoted to god of the sea (as Neptune Oceanus). Neptune Oceanus was often depicted surfing on a sea shell towed by "sea horses" i.e., hippocampi, half horses and half fish (as the Romans were practical even in their most fanciful moments, the front half of these remarkable beings were horses, the back half fish). Neptune was equated with Poseidon and assumed his characteristics, but he was far less popular among Romans than Poseidon was with Greeks, who had a fondness for the sea that the Romans never pretended to share. However, Vergil stresses his majesty, his awesome power, and his benevolent qualities, attributing all the *Aeneid*'s considerable collection of aquatic nastiness to Juno and her occasional henchmen such as Aeolus, King of the Winds. When Aeolus at the behest of Juno stirred a mighty tempest on the sea,

Vergil says that Neptune raised his great head calmly above the waters, rebuked the winds, calmed the turbulent waves, drove away the storm clouds, and brought back the sun. Then he drove his horses, with their bronze hooves and golden manes, across a suddenly quiet sea, bringing peace and beauty as he moved. (*Aeneid I, 124-156*). Later during Aeneas' turbulent adventures, after reassuring a tearful Venus with promises concerning Aeneas' safe arrival in Italy, Neptune yoked his foaming horses with a gold yoke and guided his flying chariot lightly over the waves, reducing the raging sea to calm under his thundering axle tree. As he advanced, the storm dissipated and the minor sea deities, accompanied by a whale or two, played round his car. (*Aeneid V, 816-826*) The Romans, who always kept a wary eye on the sea and never felt at home on it, preferred to think of Neptune as quieting the waters; they had a strong feeling that somebody needed to.

4. A. Pluto/Hades, God of the Underworld

As usual with classical deities, Pluto had a variety of names. In his case, largely because people were afraid to pronounce his chief one, Hades, there was more difficulty than usual. The ancient *Hymn to Demeter* coyly calls him the Lord of Many, or the Host of Many, referring to the multitudes of the dead over whom he ruled. Evidently, because he was overlord of the dead, no one wanted to invite his attention, lest he be looking for more subjects to add to his realm. (This complicated matters when offerings were made to him, as the person making the sacrifice of an unfortunate black animal turned his face away. Why they made offerings to him and tried to avoid his attention simultaneously is never explained. This whole weird business gives new meaning to the term mystery religion.)

He was usually referred to as Pluto, a name which most mythologists connect with riches, as did the Romans, who called him Dis (the Rich One) as well as Pluto and (if deemed absolutely necessary) Hades. (The Romans, ever practical, said that if his realm began at the Earth's crust he must needs own all the mineral deposits and other nice things found under that crust, thus the name Dis. A bit later in this tome we will find the goddess Demeter closely connected with someone else named Pluto or Plutus, but this is no place to go into all that). Everyone agrees that he was the brother of Zeus and Poseidon and shared the lordship of the world with them, his share being the underworld. As though he wasn't already intimidating enough, he had a helmet of darkness that either made him invisible or allowed him to see at night.

Pluto's dismal realm was located underground and was separated from the land of the living by five rivers, none of which were placid little streams– these were Phlegethon, the river of fire, Acheron, the river of woe, Cocytus, the river of lamentation, and Lethe, the river of forgetfulness. Number Five was the Styx, the river of the unbreakable oath, surrounding the whole enclave with its dark waters. According to Vergil, the boatman Charon plied his trade at the joining of Acheron and Cocytus. This redoubtable mariner was old, unkempt, and dirty, but his flaming eyes and obvious strength dared anybody to start anything. Although his appearance was definitely unappealing, as he poled up to the bank he was besieged by scores of dead people who wanted to get across to Hades, where all the deceased of the ancient world, good, bad, or indifferent, were supposed to go. If they lacked the proper credentials, however, such as a burial and a bit of passage money, they had to wander around as ghosts until somebody helped them out or a hundred years had passed; otherwise, Charon wouldn't oblige them. On each trip, he chose a few of the properly certified, shooed the rest away, and rowed back across the boiling, muddy stream. Once accepted by Charon, the dead still weren't home free. He whisked them across and deposited them in the oozing mud on the far side, where they trudged through the goo keeping a wary eye on Cerberus, the beloved watchdog of Pluto. Cerberus was a huge canine (more or less), with three heads and a dragon's tail. Around each of his three necks was a mane of hissing snakes, all of whom writhed as Cerberus, in the manner of dogs, barked his three heads off. He lay beside the actual entrance to inner Hades, and his assignment was to keep those inside Hades in and unacceptable visitors out. He had very little trouble doing so, as nobody really wanted to find out what he might do if challenged. Just past Cerberus' station, three judges, Aeacus, Minos and Rhadamanthus, decided the fate of souls: heroes went to the Elysian Fields; evildoers to Tartarus. Those who didn't really fit in either category went, according to Vergil, to a number of pigeon-holes in between. On the right (of course, since literature has long had something against all things on the left) was the path to Elysium, eternal home of the blessed, and to the left was the triple wall of Tartarus, eternal home of the definitely unblessed. Around that triple wall roared Phlegethon, River of Fire. The wall was breached by a gate of adamantine, the hardest substance known to the ancient world. The gate-tower was of iron, and atop it perched one of the Furies, (those female demon-deities who had snakes for hair and eyes that wept tears of blood and were sent to punish the guilty). This one was Tisiphone, who outdid even her sisters in Extreme Nastiness. She sat guarding the gate day and night, pulling her bloody robe around her and refusing to take a coffee break or even a short nap. From beyond the walls came sounds of lashes, clanking iron, dragging chains, and, as might have been expected, groans. Rhadamanthus, the most inflexible of Hades' three judges, made the inmates of Tartarus confess their evil deeds and assigned imaginative punishments as just recompense. These punishments differed in many respects, but they were all exceedingly unpleasant.

The blessed dead who went to the Elysian Fields fared better. In Elysium, unlike the gloomy grey atmosphere of the rest of Hades, sunlight and green plants existed. The blessed souls of heroes and public benefactors danced, sang, wrestled, worked out with weights, and probably got in a few rounds of golf, as they could do all the things they had enjoyed in life.

Pluto, God of the Dead

Pluto, as all classical gods seemed to do, longed for feminine companionship. Women were understandably reluctant to receive his addresses; he gave new meaning to the phrase holy terror. He was huge, strong, stern and dark, he smelled slightly of sulphur, and his home hardly sounded inviting, considering where it was located. His palace down in the underworld was described only as being many-gated, surrounded by wide wastelands and pale meadows of flowering asphodel. (Nobody knew exactly what that was, and marriageable maidens were not eager to find out).

The myths agree that Pluto fell madly in love with Persephone, daughter of Zeus and the grain goddess Demeter (yes, Hesiod left her out of his major list of Zeus' **inamoratae**, but we'll get to her story later). Some say Pluto, having seen the glowing maiden, asked Zeus for her and received a tacit permission, which neither of them bothered to mention to her powerful mother. (If he did actually ask fatherly permission to approach a maiden he craved, Pluto was surely unique in the annals of classical divine lovers). Even if he did ask Zeus' permission, he certainly didn't consult Persephone. Everyone agrees that he sprang, in his dark chariot with its rusty reins, from his underworld realm and carried her off as she was picking flowers (a notoriously unsafe occupation that was the undoing of more than one mythological maiden). Exactly where the dangerous flowers were located, though, is a problem. Pausanias (*Description of Greece I, 38:5*) says that Pluto carried Persephone through a cave at Eleusis beside the stream Cephisus. Diodorus Siculus (*V, 3*) however, quoting from Carcinus the tragic poet who visited often in Syracuse, states flatly that the abduction of Persephone took place in the Sicilian territory of Enna, where the meadows known for beautiful flowers, especially violets, were favorite haunts of Demeter and her daughter Persephone. Diodorus, who had a poet's fondness for hyperbole, said that the meadows smelled so sweet that trained hunting dogs could not hold the trail, as their keen noses were overcome by the fragrance. However that may have been, these charming meadows lay much too near certain sacred groves, and Pluto, chariot and all, suddenly swooped out upon Persephone and her flower-gathering companions. Ovid in *Metamorphoses V* sides with Diodorus and declares that the foul deed took place in Sicily. All sources agree that the terrified girl called on her mother and her companions, but there was no rescue. Ovid credits both the nymph Cyane (who was so upset by her failure to help that she wept herself into a spring) and Arethusa (who evidently at this time had already been changed from nymph to waterworks) with trying to interfere but to no avail. The Homeric *Hymn to Demeter* circa 650-550 BCE says that Helios the Sun saw all, and would later carry the tale to Demeter.

Pluto was successful in his abduction, and Persephone became the Queen of the Dead, the one whose name may not be mentioned (Diodorus), to whom such charming offerings as a sterile cow were made (*Aeneid, VI*). As we shall see when we come to the story of her mother, Persephone's tenure in Dis' gloomy palace was at least not year-round.

However reluctant a bride Persephone may have been, she took the usual wifely dim view of Pluto's occasionally wandering eye. When he fell in love with Leuce, the "white one," one of those ubiquitous daughters of Oceanus and Tethys, he carried her off to the Underworld in his usual style. She soon died, with or without a bit of assistance from Persephone. Hades changed her into a white poplar tree, which he placed in the Elysian Fields. From this tree Heracles gathered the garland for his head when he was roaming about in the Underworld. Pluto also fell in love with Minthe, another nymph. He leaped out of his chariot (which he had evidently furbished up a bit, as it is described in this myth as golden) and impressed her greatly, but before anything really interesting could happen Persephone found out and turned Minthe into the herb, mint.

4. B. Roman Pluto

The Romans paid as little attention to Pluto/Hades/Dis as they politely could. Ceres and not Pluto is the twelfth of the Roman Dii Consentes. He and Proserpina (the Latin name of Persephone) were known as the Dii Inferi, Gods of the Underworld (Inferus). They symbolized the power of the Earth to provide human beings the necessities for living, as Proserpina was the Spring Maiden (a fact we shall go into later) and Dis controlled the riches underground as well as the Inferus, the home of the dead. Strangely enough Pax, the Roman goddess who was the personification of peace, in her well-equipped temple in Rome was depicted with an untipped spear, holding an olive twig in her hand and the young Pluto in her arm. Whether the Romans thought that Pluto God of Riches or Pluto God of the Dead was connected with peace they left unspecified; either seems a bit of a stretch.

The Romans associated Pluto with the least appealing aspects of their terrain. Near the shrine of Apollo at Cumae lie Lake Avernus and the Burning Fields, two forbidding and extremely smelly geographical features involving boiling mud, spewing gases, and the cheerful yellow fluorescence and strong odor of abundant sulphur. This dismal spot was proclaimed to be an entrance to Hades, the World of the Dead.

5. A. Hestia, Goddess of the Hearth

Hestia, the Greek goddess of the Hearth or Fireplace, was the sister of Zeus, Hera, Poseidon, and Pluto, but her history was one step more outlandish than her siblings. The first-born offspring of Cronus and Rhea, she was the first to be swallowed by Cronus and the last to be given back; thus she was known as the first and the last of his children. (This bizarre biographical bit is sometimes said to be the reason why the Greeks gave her offerings at the beginning and the end of their meals; another possible sidelight on this custom will be offered a bit further on).

However difficult her beginning, she was central to Greek life; the hearth or fireplace which was her special domain was the all-important source of warmth and light and cooking and the symbol of the home and of life itself, around which each new-born child was carried before being received into the family. Hestia was no less important in civic life: each city had a public hearth sacred to her, where the fire was never allowed to go out. If a colony was to be founded, the colonist carried with them coals from the hearth of the mother city with which to kindle the fire on the new city's hearth, which they promptly dedicated to Hestia.

In spite of the signal honors paid her, she was the quietest and gentlest of the Great Twelve. (Perhaps her peculiar birth [births?] had made her shy, although their bizarre heritage did not have such a beneficial effect on her siblings.) It has been mentioned that she was the only Olympian who took no part in Hera's revolt. Plato makes Socrates say (*Phaedrus 246e*) that when Zeus and all the other Olympians go out to wage a war; Hestia alone remains in the house of the gods. As domestic Commander in Chief, she would certainly have plenty to do, keeping the home fires burning and protecting the plethora of orphans and missing children which all that warring tends to produce.

Some disgruntled souls attribute her gentle graciousness to the fact that she was immune to the spells of Aphrodite; however, she shared this unusual blessing with Athena and Artemis, neither of whom seemed the milder for it. When Poseidon and Apollo both demanded to wed her, she touched the head of Zeus and swore to remain a maiden. Zeus, greatly pleased (and perhaps relieved that he was not called upon to arbitrate that little dispute), honored her with the place in the middle of the house (where the fire in archaic times was located). Perhaps for this reason or the one mentioned earlier, she also received the first and last portion of offerings, so that every meal began and ended with an offering to her.

Hestia's worship was ubiquitous; in every temple she was honored by the fire placed there. (*Homeric Hymn 5*). As she spent her time alleviating the many cares of mortals, and shunned the high-jinks of Aphrodite, she didn't make it into the livelier myths. There is one story that the lusty demi-god

Priapus tried to sneak up on her with amorous intent while she slept, but a donkey braying awakened her; thus the lowly donkey became her animal.

Homeric Hymn 29 extols her importance and invokes her aid. "Hestia, in the high places of all, both immortal gods and men who walk on earth, you hold the highest honor: your portion and your right is glorious indeed. For there are no mortal banquets where one does not duly pour a libation of sweet wine to Hestia both first and last ... Hestia, holy and dear, come and dwell in this glorious house in friendship ... being aware of the noble actions of men, increase their wisdom and their strength."

Vesta carrying a torch

5. B. Roman Vesta

Vesta, Hestia's counterpart, was one of the most popular and mysterious goddesses of the Roman pantheon. Not much is known of her origin, except that she was goddess of the hearth, which was the centre of the Roman home. Every day, during a meal, Romans threw a small cake on the fire for Vesta. Good luck was assured if it burned with a crackle, so wise housewives probably chose its ingredients to assure that it would.

The worship of Vesta, like much of Roman worship, originated in the home, but quite early her worship evolved into a state cult set up by King Numa Pompilius (715-673 BCE), who established the Vestal Virgins (*Livy I, 20*) to keep her home fire burning, as she was protector of the sacred flame that was said to have been brought from Troy to Italy by the hero Aeneas. This fire was relit every March 1st from a coal of the old one and had to be kept alight all year. In her shrine was also the sacred Palladium, a small wooden statue of Minerva, which Aeneas supposedly brought from Troy. According to legend, if anything ever happened to either of these, disaster would fall on Rome. The worship of Vesta declined after Constantine adopted Christianity as the state religion, and in 382 CE.Gratian (one of the less appealing later Emperors) confiscated the Atrium Vestae. Disaster did indeed fall on Rome, but this probably had more to do with Gratian's featherheaded policies than with Vesta's sacred fire.

Vesta was a quiet well-behaved goddess, never joining in the endless arguments and fights of the other gods. When that Johnny-Come-Lately, Bacchus, demanded a spot among the Dii Consentes, Vesta gave him hers. She had probably had more than enough of the divine soap opera constantly going on in that august assembly.

6. A. Athena, Goddess of Wisdom

Athena was the Greek goddess of wisdom, the arts, handicrafts, and almost everything else that took a great deal of intelligence, as only Apollo among the Olympians came close to rivaling her in that admirable quality. As we have mentioned before, she was the daughter of Zeus alone as he had an anxiety attack and, evidently fearing that his consort Metis (Wisdom) would bear an offspring he could not control, swallowed his unfortunate inamorata. Later he developed a headache (which seems a strange result for such a dietary aberration; but then, the whole story is lacking in medical logic). The ever-helpful blacksmith god Hephaestus split his skull open (and, in the light of Hephaestus' own story, which we shall consider later, probably thoroughly enjoyed doing so). As a result of this rough and ready surgical technique Athena emerged, fully grown and wearing armor. This might have been a sad omen for what her major occupation would be, but, though fierce and brave in battle, she was interested only in wars to defend the state and home. Her efforts in this direction were helped by the fact that she was Zeus's favorite child and was allowed to use his weapons, including his thunderbolt. Athena also wore upon her breastplate the aegis, a protective device that was originally associated with Zeus, but later the sole property of Athena. This shining shield became even more powerful when, as we shall see, she received the snaky head of Medusa to fasten in the middle of it.

One legend says that Medusa acquired that snaky head because of hubris, which the Greek gods considered the greatest of all Cardinal Sins and of which Athena, as the story of Medusa indicates, took a particularly dim view. (Hubris consisted of an overweening arrogance concerning one's own outstanding qualities combined with the incredible stupidity required to challenge the gods with those qualities. Admittedly a lovely specimen, Medusa had compared herself in beauty to Athena with appalling results). Arachne of Lydia was also a beautiful maiden (of which ancient Greece seems to have had an endless supply), who took extreme pride not in her beauty but in her skill. As she was a better weaver than anyone in Lydia, which was a land famous for marvelous textiles, she was harebrained enough to announce to the world in general that she was as good a weaver as Athena was, if not better. Athena appeared to her in the guise of an old woman and warned her not to boast, but no improvement in her behavior resulted. Athena then accepted the challenge, and the two sat down to weave. When the contest was done, Athena was enraged to see that Arachne's tapestry was in no way inferior to her own. (It was bad enough to boast of matching the gods, but even worse to make good that boast.) When the fury of the goddess blazed forth, Arachne hanged herself. Athena, perhaps feeling that she had gone a bit overboard, changed her into a spider so that she could continue to use her matchless skill (and incidentally could be deprived of her boastful tongue and lovely body).

Athena was often the patroness of heroes; without her Odysseus would never have made it home to Ithaca in the face of Poseidon's wrath. (For that matter, he would probably never have made it through the Trojan War or dreamed up all that horse business without her assistance.) Her interest in the male sex was purely maternal, however, as she was foremost among the three virgin Goddesses unphased by the wiles of Aphrodite, and was known as the Maiden, Parthenos. From this word was taken the name of the most important Temple dedicated to her, the Parthenon of Athens. Her immunity to the tender passion did not make her any less vain of her looks than other females, however: she invented the flute but threw it away because her face was distorted when she played it. Athens was of course her namesake and her city, and the olive she created in the contest with Poseidon her tree. The owl evidently gained its reputation for wisdom solely because it was her bird; under careful observance, owls exhibit no special signs of intellectual acumen.

6. B. Roman Minerva

The Roman goddess Minerva or Menerva, like Jupiter and Juno, the other two members of the Capitoline Triad, was evidently of Etruscan origin. Since she was the daughter of Jupiter and Juno and the virgin goddess of wisdom, presiding over learning, all handicrafts, inventions, arts and sciences, she was equated to Athena. As usual, the Romans gave Minerva many attributes and names. As Minerva Victrix she was goddess of war. As Minerva Medica she was patroness of physicians. As she was also the inventor of numbers and musical instruments, Ovid had good reason to call her the "goddess of a thousand works." Like most of the Roman gods, she spent more time working and less time interacting with individual mortals than did her Greek counterpart. Minerva was Goddess of wisdom and learning, meditation, inventiveness, accomplishments, the arts, spinning and weaving, and commerce. Possibly because of all these spheres of influence, Minerva has many aspects, attributes, names and epithets.

7. A. Phoebus Apollo, God of the Sun

Apollo and his twin sister, Artemis, products of one of Zeus' amours, were born to Latona or Leto on the island of Delos, a barren and unprepossessing little rock which wasn't even anchored, but tossed around in the sea. Leto, an outcast because earth and heaven feared the jealous wifely rage of Hera, approached this bit of terra not very firma as she wandered about growing closer and closer to her delivery time. Goddess and island had a little chat, the upshot of which was Leto's promise that her prospective son Apollo would not despise the barren little isle, (which was never going to give any competition to the Garden of Eden) but on the contrary would have a great shrine there if it were to be his birthplace. As the little island offered a welcome to the distressed mother-to-be, four pillars immediately rose from the bottom of the sea and anchored it forever, and the welfare of both pregnant lady and despised island were assured. (*Homeric Hymn to Apollo, 51-88*)

In Greece and in Rome Phoebus Apollo had only one name (or pair of names), but he had multiple duties. He became god of the sun (a post that Homer indicates that he usurped from the older Helios), light, truth, music, and medicine.

Like Poseidon, Apollo had his good moods and his bad moods. He played a golden lyre, but he also shot arrows from a silver bow, evidently with unsettling accuracy, as he is called the Far Shooter. The Roman poet Horace says, with a philosophical shrug, "Sometimes Apollo plays the lyre; sometimes he bends the bow." (*Odes II, 10: 16-20*)

His prophecies were much sought by mortals, because as god of truth and light he could not tell a lie. (This must have been a serious handicap when dealing with some humans and all the Olympians. Apollo understandably employed the method later adopted by multitudes of lawyers and schoolboys–he never gave anybody a straight answer.) When only a few days old, (gods grow up quickly) he slew a mighty Python which lived at Delphi beside the Castalian Spring, and took over the shrine of Delphi, where he proceeded to deal with this mortal passion for truth. (Some Romanticists who love those endless metamorphosis stories said that Castalia was a nymph whom Apollo loved who fled from him and dived into the spring which was then named after her. However that may have been, water from this spring was sacred; it was used to purify visitors and inspire poets, two groups of people who need all the purification and inspiration they can get).

As god of the sun Apollo drove his four horses of fire, yoked to his golden, gem-laden chariot, across the sky daily, sinking into the ocean at sunset. (Where he found time for slaying serpents and chasing girls in the midst of this extremely demanding work schedule is one of those Olympian mysteries).

Unlike his uncles Poseidon and Pluto and his father Zeus, Apollo was a fine beardless specimen of early manhood. He had all their fondness for the ladies, however, and, although he had no official wife, he had loves aplenty. Strangely enough, not all the objects of his attention were thrilled. Daphne, daughter of the river god Peneus, was one of those beautiful (aren't they always?) devotees of the virgin goddess Artemis. When Apollo approached her, she ran from him. This attempt to outrun a god was a singularly hopeless effort, and as she felt his breath on the back of her neck, she cried to her father for help. To Apollo's considerable surprise, he cast his arms around, not a soft young maiden, but a rough young tree trunk. Finding himself with a firm hold on a laurel tree, Apollo sighed and made it his official symbol.

Undismayed by this evidence that the path of true (and sometimes untrue) love seldom runs smoothly, Apollo loved Coronis, the daughter of Phlegyas, King of the Lapiths, and she bore him Asclepius. According to Pindar Coronis fell in love with a mortal, and the crow, one of Apollo's feathered friends, told on her (for which the ungrateful Apollo turned its snowy feathers black). Apollo sent Artemis to kill his faithless love, but he rescued his son and gave the boy to his uncle, the scholarly centaur Chiron, to be brought up. Asclepius developed such medicinal skills that he could even raise the dead, and Pluto complained to Zeus of coming population (or depopulation) problems. Zeus took care of the matter by killing Asclepius with one of his thunderbolts. Grieving, furious, but too clever to confront Zeus directly, Apollo turned his anger on the Cyclopes who had made the lightning bolts. This tactic didn't work: Zeus promptly made Apollo a mortal and sent him off to serve King Admetus of Pherae. Apollo eventually regained his godhood, returned to Olympus, and successfully persuaded Zeus (who was feeling by now that he might possibly have overreacted) to resurrect Asclepius and transform him into a full Olympian -- the god of medicine.

Some of the more gossip-prone ancients claimed that Troilius, son of Queen Hecuba of Troy, was a son of Apollo. Whether or not that was the case, Apollo fell in love with Cassandra, the daughter of Hecuba and her husband Priam, and gave her the ability to foretell the future. Cassandra (who didn't even have devotion to Artemis as an excuse) rejected him, and the enraged god, unable to retract his gift, arranged matters so that her prophecies would never be believed by anyone. Thus the poor girl foretold the destruction of Troy, the murders both of Agamemnon, the Greek commander who captured her, and herself-- all to no avail. Nobody seemed to notice that her prophecies had an eerie way of coming true.

In another bizarre story, Apollo fell in love with a princess named Leucothea, daughter of Orchamus, rousing the jealous of Leucothea's sister Clytie (Clytia). Clytie would gladly have received Apollo's addresses, but gods like men generally want what they cannot have, and he wasn't interested. Clytie sat wasting away, watching his daily trip across the sky, until Apollo changed her into a sunflower, which still follows the path of the sun every day.

All this amorous intrigue not withstanding, Apollo also took a lively interest in various mortal combats such as the Trojan War. The *Iliad* opened with a bang as Chryses, an elderly priest of Apollo whose daughter had been filched by the Greek commander Agamemnon, prayed to Apollo to avenge Agamemnon's refusal to give the girl back. Enthusiastically embracing his priest's request, Apollo mowed down the Greeks for nine days with those arrows of his, until Achilles held a meeting and insisted that Agamemnon be sensible about all this. Agamemnon angrily returned the maiden, but he took over a girl whom Achilles had filched, after which Achilles pouted in his tent watching the Greeks lose for a while.

In this memorable war Apollo played another part, without which the Roman race might have died aborning. When Diomedes injured the Trojan hero Aeneas in battle, Aeneas' mother Aphrodite tried to rescue him, but Diomedes injured her as well. Apollo looked over the scene, enveloped Aeneas in a cloud, and took him to a sacred spot in Troy where Artemis healed him. Thanks to this timely intervention of Apollo, Aeneas survived to lead the remnants of the Trojans to Italy, where Apollo proceeded to help Aeneas carve out a home that would eventually produce the Romans.

Apollo shared Athena's views on hubris. When Queen Niobe of Thebes boasted that she had borne fourteen children and thus was superior to Leto since she had only two, Apollo and his twin sister Artemis, both excellent archers, avenged the insult to their mother by killing the sons and daughters of Niobe. (Niobe reacted to this backset by turning into a stone, which is still eternally wet with her tears.)

Lesser gods, as well as mortals, could come to grief through hubris. Marsyas was a satyr, one of the race of demi-gods who were half man and half goat. He had the misfortune to find on the ground that flute that Athena invented and then tossed away. He played on it so beautifully that he ran completely amuck and challenged Apollo to a contest of music. He lost the contest and soon afterward his skin. He was flayed alive in a cave near Calaenae in Phrygia for his hubris in challenging a god. His blood turned into the river Marsyas. (Most of the waterways, and a number of geographical features, of the Mediterranean world seem to have been demi-gods or people at one time or another).

Pan, the chief satyr whose story will be told later, once had the audacity to compare his music with that of Apollo, and to challenge Apollo to a trial of skill. The unfortunate King Midas was chosen as judge of this contest, and he was delighted when Pan blew his rustic melody on his Pan pipe or Syrinx. After Apollo played his golden lyre, Midas, with a lamentable taste in music and an even more lamentable misunderstanding of politics, declared Pan the winner. Apollo said that such ears as Midas' should have a suitable shape, and thereafter the poor king had donkey ears.

Apollo's love and pity could also be stirred, however, as they were when his mortal son Phaethon came to his sun palace, very small and squinting in the blinding light, but determined to ask Apollo for proof of his parentage, because some smart-aleck school fellows had laughed at his claim to be the son of Apollo and had called both Phaethon and his mother some indelicate names. Not being well acquainted with the perils of fatherhood, Apollo rashly swore by the Styx to give the boy whatever proof he desired. Anyone acquainted with the tastes of young mortals could have predicted the outcome -- Phaethon, picturing himself sailing across the heavens in full view of those big-mouth boys, asked to drive Apollo's blazing chariot for a day. In vain did Apollo plead and promise rich gifts and outline the perils of guiding horses of fire around the Crab and the Scorpion and the other grisly Zodiac signs. Phaethon was stubborn as only young boys can be, and the Styx oath was unbreakable. As might have been expected, Phaethon proved unequal to the task, and when he dropped the reins in panic the fiery horses started a merry little conflagration everywhere they dipped near the earth, creating the Sahara desert and causing the Nile river to go hide its head. Zeus had little choice but to zap another of Apollo's sons, but this time grief and guilt, not anger, were Apollo's reactions. The Roman poet Ovid tells this story in a very touching way, but, as he can never be serious for more than fifteen lines at a time, he adds that Phaethon "fell out of a great adventure." (*Metamorphoses II. 328*)

Like the other Olympians, Apollo's majesty and might were not lessened by his peccadilloes or misfortunes. "Like a star at noonday, the lord, far-shooting Apollo, leaped forth: great flashes of fire, whose brightness reached to heaven, flew from him. As he entered his shrine he caused a flame between the priceless tripods to flare up bright, showing the splendor of his shafts so that their radiance filled all Crisa, and this outburst of Phoebus cast great fear upon the Crisaeans. From his shrine he sprang forth again, swift as a thought, bearing the form of a man, brisk and sturdy, in the prime of his youth, while his broad shoulders were covered with his hair." (*Homeric Hymn to Apollo*: *440-451*)

7. B. Roman Apollo

In Roman religion, Apollo was worshiped in various forms, most significantly as a god of healing and of prophecy, yet clothed in all the splendor proper to the light of the world. Ovid in the story of Phaethon pictures him clothed in purple and seated on a throne carved of a vast emerald, wearing the rays of the sun as his crown. In art he was portrayed as the perfection of youth and beauty. One of the most celebrated depictions of him is the Apollo Belvedere, a marble statue in the Belvedere of the Vatican.

According to some legends Apollo and Iris, goddess of the rainbow, were parents of the door god Janus, guardian to the Roman peoples.

Apollo was also responsible for the famous Cumaean Sibyl. There were ten Sibyls, or prophetesses of Apollo, scattered throughout the classical Mediterranean World, but the most respected of these in Italy lived at Cumae near Naples. Apollo, in one of his impressionable moods, fell in love with her, and she asked to live as many years as she could hold grains of sand in her hands. He granted her wish, but when she was unwise enough to deny him her favors, he refused to attach eternal youth to her years and she grew incredibly shriveled and longed for death. Evidently going into deep depression, or perhaps a major fit of the sulks, she simply wrote her prophecies on leaves, which she then placed at the mouth of her cave. Whether anyone saw them was evidently no concern of hers, but she eventually decided to create an album, the Sibylline Books, which she brought to the Roman king Tarquinius Superbus for purchase. The unfortunate outcome of that affair will be recounted in the section on Roman temples.

7. C. Mithras

This late-comer, evidently compiled from various sources, is even harder than most of the classical deities to pin down. Mithras was identified with the Greek sun god Helios in the first century BCE. Called Mihr in middle Persian, he was the Zoroastrian Sun God. As a sun representative with the title Invictus, a reputation for fidelity, manliness and bravery, and a passion for discipline, he was especially attractive to soldiers and sometimes the disadvantaged. Plutarch wrote that the pirates of Cilicia were practicing secret rites of Mithras around 67 BCE, and he is convinced that their rites spread to Rome. Whatever his origins, Roman soldiers involved in the suppression of the Jewish revolt of 60-70 CE dedicated offerings to Mithras on their return home. Wise men or magi from King Tiridates of Armenia, evidently spotting an opportunity and pouncing on it, proclaimed that the Emperor Nero was an emanation of Mithras. As anyone acquainted with that far from humble emperor could have expected, Nero promptly decided to be initiated in their mysteries. Considering the homeland of these ambassadors, Mithraism began to share in the official recognition that had been granted quite some time before to Phrygian deities such as Cybele. From this time on Mithras was usually shown in a Phrygian cap. The poet Statius in his Thebaid Book I, line 719-20 mentions his worship as well-established in 80 CE.

Various stories survive to account for Mithras' birth. Often he is depicted springing from the living rock or from a tree; at Hadrian's Wall, however, a sculpture shows Mithras bursting from the Cosmic Egg, holding in his upraised hands the Sword of Truth and Torch of Light. Around him are the Twelve Signs of the Zodiac in an egg-shaped frame. The idea of a cosmic or world Egg from which life was created is very widely distributed, appearing in Chinese mythology, Sanskrit scriptures, Egyptian religion and even Finnish mythology. The idea that he was born of a virgin on December 25 appears to have developed later, perhaps in order to rival Christianity.

Whatever his origins, after a youth of hardship he captured a bull, evidently a primaeval figure, and dragged it into a cave, where he killed it in order to use its life force for humanity. From the body of the bull grew plants and herbs, vines came from its blood, and from its semen all useful animals. This bull slaying scene - known as a tauroctony -was to be found in relief or as a wall painting in all Mithraea. The scene includes the Sun god and the Moon goddess as well as the Raven, the Sun god's messenger. Mithras, the representative or Son of the Sun, is attended by a dog, a snake and a scorpion, as well as by the twin Torchbearers, Cautes and Cautopates. These torchbearers are sometimes interpreted as light and darkness or, in an astrological vein, the equinoxes. The most picturesque interpretation is that Cautes with uplifted torch represents the rising sun and therefore hope, while Cautopates with a down-turned torch represents the setting sun and sorrow. All the figures are clothed in the costume of ancient Persia, including the Phrygian cap.

8. A. Artemis, Goddess of the Moon and Hunting

Apollo's twin Artemis was said to have been born before him. In some of the more bizarre legends, she got an early start on her role as guardian of young children and patron of women in childbirth by helping to deliver her twin. As Apollo was the sun god, largely replacing the older Helios, Artemis became goddess of the moon, gaining that goddess's name of Selene and often being depicted wearing a crescent moon over her forehead. However, she was chiefly goddess of the wilderness, the hunt and wild animals, armed with bow and arrows made by Hephaestus and the Cyclopes. Like her brother, she had a multi-faceted personality; she both hunted and protected wild animals. At an early age (in one legend she was three years old) Artemis like her aunt Hestia asked her father Zeus to grant her eternal virginity, and when she took up outdoor sports she was accompanied by a train of nymphs, who like her were sworn to chastity. Thus as she grew up and began to roam the forests, hunters had to beware, not only of wild boar and disgruntled bears, but of any pool from which they could hear giggling and splashing. When an unwary young hunter named Actaeon happened upon Artemis and her nymphs bathing in a pool, the stunned young man understandably stopped and stared. When Artemis saw him, she transformed him into a stag and set his own hounds upon him. Acting upon conventional wisdom "if it looks like a stag and runs like a stag ..." the dogs chased him down and killed him.

As Artemis was fierce in protecting her own chastity, so she expected the same from her followers. Elsewhere in this tome is recorded the sad fate of Artemis' nymph Callisto, who, having received no sympathy from the goddess after being outwitted by Zeus, wound up a constellation.

Like Zeus, Artemis seems to have decorated the sky with those unfortunate enough to love her. When the giant hunter Orion tried to make love to Artemis, she killed him with her bow and arrows and added one more constellation to the heavens. An even more star-studded version of this legend says that the offended goddess conjured up a scorpion that killed Orion and his dog. The scorpion was then transformed into the constellation Scorpio, Orion became the constellation that bears his name, and his dog became Sirius, the dogstar.

Artemis also gave short shrift to anyone mistreating her sacred animals, as Agamemnon discovered just before setting out to wage the Trojan War when he or some of his men killed a stag in her sacred grove. His ships were becalmed, and the seer Calchas said that Artemis would only bring back the winds if Agamemnon sacrificed his daughter Iphigenia. Some myths say he did sacrifice Iphigenia, others that Artemis put a deer in her place and took Iphigenia away as her priestess.

She had the usual divine contempt for hubris; we have already recorded the sad fate of the children of the arrogant Queen Niobe.

Artemis was always goddess of contradictions; although the arrows of Artemis brought women sudden death while giving they were giving birth, she was the guardian of young things, and the protectress of women in labor. Perhaps this association with childbirth explains why Artemis, the virgin goddess of hunting and wildlife, running lightly in her silver sandals carrying her bow and arrows, underwent a major change in Asia Minor. The cult statues of the Ephesian Artemis are those of a fertility goddess, standing erect, her chest covered with numerous breasts (or protuberances of some sort; scholars have a field day arguing over exactly what sort).

As has been mentioned, Artemis was confused with Selene, the moon goddess, as her brother Apollo superseded Selene's brother Helios. Selene originally was a young woman dressed in a robe, not hunting gear, who wore a crescent moon on her forehead and carried a torch. The most famous story about her is that she fell in love with a young shepherd named Endymion and kept him sleeping forever in a cave so that she could visit him at night, a tale which certainly does not fit in with Artemis' determined virginity.

Getting mixed up with Selene was bad enough. Even more appalling was Artemis' identification with another goddess left over from the Titan age, Hecate. This dread goddess of the crossroads was not only usually accompanied by her two ghost hounds, but also was sometimes depicted as having three heads; one of a dog, one of a snake and one of a horse. (This bizarre anatomy enabled her to look three ways at once and keep abreast of affairs; hence she was to be found at the spot where three roads meet, with each of her watchful heads facing in a certain direction). The natural habitat of this unsightly goddess of ghosts and queen of witches was Hades, and when Persephone was kidnapped by Pluto, Hecate befriended the captured and bewildered girl .The ancient *Homeric Hymn to Demeter* explains that "tender-hearted Hecate" heard the maiden's cries. (Tender-hearted toward wronged females, be they maidens like Persephone or witches like her servants Circe and Medea, [6] she undoubtedly was, but the revenge she took on their masculine tormentors was sometimes a bit over the top).

Some scholars try to bring a bit of order into all this chaos by identifying Artemis as the waxing moon or maiden, Selene as the full moon or matron, and Hecate as the waning moon, the dark of the moon, or the crone.

8. B. Roman Diana

Diana, twin sister of Apollo, was goddess of the moon; her name is possibly derived from 'diviana' ("the shining one"). First and foremost, however, she was the protector of wild animals and forests. Under Greek influence she was equated with Artemis, whom she resembled so closely, not only as huntress and moon divinity but also as a goddess of fertility who could give women both fertility and easy births. She was essentially a goddess of the woodlands: her sanctuaries were commonly in groves; all groves, especially those of oak, were sacred to her. She was praised for her youthful strength, athletic grace, beauty, and last but not least her hunting skills. With two other deities, Egeria the water nymph, her servant and assistant midwife, and Virbius, a woodland Italian divinity, she made up one of those trinities the Romans were so fond of. She had a train of virgin nymphs, some of whom, such as Camilla [7], indulged not only in hunting but in warfare. Powerless to keep her followers from the perils of war,

Diana, Roman Goddess of Hunting

Diana made very sure that those who killed the girls paid for it. She was typically depicted as young huntress, usually carrying a bow and arrows, which like her brother she could use with devastating accuracy.

9. A. Aphrodite, Goddess of Love

All Olympians could cause mischief, but none on quite so grand a scale as the Goddess of Love. From the moment Aphrodite (Foam Born) rose naked from the Sea on a scallop shell (evidently full-grown and ready for action), she was trouble. The ancient *Homeric Hymn to Aphrodite* credits the Hours with decking this damp phenomenon of pulchritude in gorgeous garments and gold jewelry, which only added to her incredible appeal. According to Hesiod she was blown by the gentle East Wind to the island of Cythera, and therefore one of her epithets was Cytherea. From that tiny island Aphrodite moved on to Cyprus, where she established herself in Paphos. Homer makes her the daughter of Zeus and Dione, who at Dodona shared an oracle and who knows what else. However this may have been, she made her way to Olympus and was welcomed there, especially by the masculine contingent.

As the goddess of love, beauty and fertility, Aphrodite was concerned with promoting the first two to bring about the third, and what happened to hapless humans (and gods) along the path to her objective never worried her. She was even more jealous of her position than most immortals. Perhaps this was because she was a latecomer to Olympus, or perhaps because her principal seats remained on the outlying islands. Her roses, myrtle trees, doves, and sparrows were a bit incongruous in intellectual Athens and certainly did not seem at home in militaristic Sparta.

Pausanias says the Spartans did their best with her, making statues of her dressed for battle, which gave her some standing in a city always in need of a high fertility rate, since most of their activities led to a high mortality rate. A tenuous understanding between her and the military Spartans might grow from the fact that Ares, the war god, was her lover. In any case, Aphrodite's primary function was to preside over reproduction, since this was essential for the survival of the community. Whatever the cause may have been, any failure to give her her due was sure to result in havoc. According to Stesichorus, (*fragment 192*: *the Palinode*) the Spartan king Tyndareus forgot her when he made sacrifices to all the gods. Aphrodite arranged for Zeus to see Leda, the beautiful queen of Sparta, bathing in the river Eurotas. Only pausing to change himself into a white swan, he swooped down, and the result was rather confusing. The stories (with the magnificent disregard for logic typical of mythology) say that Leda brought forth two eggs. One, for which Zeus was responsible, produced Helen (the future Helen of Troy) and her brother Pollux. From the other came Castor and Clytemnestra, future Queen of Mycenae. As the last two were the children of her husband Tyndareus, they were mortal. (For this, or some other reason, women swore by Castor and men by Pollux. It was always possible, of course, that in the heat of anger someone might swear by the wrong one. There are no available statistics on the results of such a faux pas for swearer or swearee).

Tyndareus, who had the doubtful privilege of acting as father protector to all these obstreperous offspring, had seen his last peaceful day. As the children grew up, Tyndareus married Clytemnestra off very respectably to Agamemnon King of Mycenae, and turned to the thorny problem of a husband for Helen, the devastatingly beautiful result of Zeus' little heart-storm which had produced Egg Number One. A regular platoon of kings, nobles, and upstarts descended on Tyndareus demanding Helen's hand in marriage. Before he named Menelaus King of Sparta as the lucky man, Tyndareus, who was no fool, made all the hopefuls swear to support Helen's husband in the quarrels that were extremely likely to arise concerning her. Every man, modestly expecting to be the winner, happily swore the oath. (A few minutes later most of them were just swearing).

Things moved relatively smoothly until Eris, goddess of Discord, who liked fireworks even if it wasn't a holiday, tossed on a banquet table on Mt. Olympus a golden apple inscribed "For the Most Beautiful." Aphrodite naturally claimed it but Hera, who took her title of Queen of Heaven very seriously, thought she had a right to all goodies, and Athena, who as goddess of wisdom should have known better, also put in a claim. Zeus was far too well acquainted with the female sex to judge this contest, so he sent them down to Mount Ida, recommending one of the sons of King Priam of Troy, Paris (one of mythology's regiment of abandoned princes who was posing as a shepherd) as an excellent judge of beauty. Somewhat startled at the sudden overpopulation of goddesses in his small glade, Paris balanced the golden apple in his hand as he listened in awe to the details of the beauty contest. The deities didn't waste time with the bathing suit and talent competitions: they got right down to the bribes. Hera promised him power over Europe and Asia; Athena, victory against the Greeks, and Aphrodite, with a slight smirk, offered the most beautiful woman in the world. Paris broke all speed records giving Aphrodite the apple. After dropping by the palace in Troy, (where he was inexplicably welcomed), he sailed away to collect his reward.

Neither Aphrodite nor Paris worried for a moment about the fact that the most beautiful woman in the world was the aforementioned Helen, the wife of King Menelaus of Sparta. The result was the Trojan War.

Aphrodite, Goddess of Love

When the lovely Atalanta wanted to avoid matrimony, (she was not, for once, a devotee of Artemis -- she was simply frightened because a pessimistic fortuneteller had informed her that marriage would be her ruin) she offered to marry the man who could outrun her in a foot race, stipulating that all who failed in this attempt should be put to death. Since she as fleet as she was beautiful, a number of rash young men came to an abrupt end trying to win her. One Hippomenes, wanting to win the prize, took the precaution of seeking Aphrodite's help with a fervent prayer. Aphrodite as usual looked with disfavor on this marriage-scorning maiden. Furthermore, (also as usual), she developed a soft spot for this young man who was not only handsome but who showed proper respect for her, and provided him with three apples of gold from her garden on Cyprus and a bit of constructive advice. Concealing the apples (considering the state in which the Greeks raced, one wonders where) he threw one in front of Atalanta each time she passed him in the race. Gathering up the apples took enough time that she lost the race and acquired a husband. In some way, this newly married pair erred and got themselves turned into lions. Some say this was through ingratitude to Venus, but others say it was because they dishonored the temple of the great Magna Mater of Asia Minor, Cybele.

One of the few mortals who got off rather lightly after scorning Aphrodite was Pygmalion, perhaps because he learned his lesson. This headstrong young sculptor lived on her own island of Cyprus, but he despised women and devoted himself to art. He decided to sculpt a perfect woman, perhaps just to show the deficiencies of the living ones. Every day the statue grew lovelier under his fingers, while Aphrodite smirked. Day by day Pygmalion grew more enamored of his creation, until he burned for a return of his love from the statue. On the next feast day of Aphrodite, Pygmalion was among the first, gift in hand, to offer his tearful supplications. After his visit to the temple, he returned home to kiss his beloved statue as usual, and to his surprise and delight she kissed him back. Aphrodite attended their wedding, and their son, Paphos, gave his name to Aphrodite's favorite city.

Aphrodite spent a good deal of time causing princesses to fall in love with handsome strangers bent on projects prejudicial to the interests of the girls' fathers, who of course were kings.

When Jason of Thessaly was sent to Colchis by his Uncle Pelias (who had usurped his brother's throne and hoped to dispose of the rightful heir), to retrieve the Golden Fleece, he asked permission of the king of Colchis to remove the Golden Fleece from the grove in which it hung. It was immediately obvious to men and gods that the king was not going to play along. So the goddess Hera, who sponsored Jason's quest, asked Aphrodite to intervene. The love goddess made the king's daughter Medea fall in love with Jason, and Medea, as recorded elsewhere in this tome, became an enthusiastic partisan of his.

King Minos of Crete also lost out because of Aphrodite's meddling. His daughter Ariadne fell in love with young Theseus of Athens as he marched by in the parade of sacrifices sent to Crete regularly to be imprisoned with the Minotaur. The result was a disappointment for Minos, who lost his bull-man, and also for Ariadne, who was deserted by Theseus on the Isle of Naxos. [8]

This was not the end of Aphrodite's meddling in the affairs of Theseus. His son Hippolytus, according to Euripides, scorned Aphrodite and, saving his prayers and offerings for Artemis, spent his time in hunting. The incensed goddess caused Hippolytus' stepmother to love him and try to seduce him. When this attempt proved to be a dismal failure, she killed herself and left a note that accused him of trying to make love to her. Theseus cursed his unfortunate son, who fled from the house and was killed by a monster. Artemis then a bit tardily presented the king with the truth.

Aphrodite's busy schedule of involving men and gods in amorous turmoil did not mean that she herself was immune to the tender passion. Various stories are told of the handsome young man Adonis, but all agree that Aphrodite loved him passionately and grieved deeply when he died young of a wound received while hunting a boar, who hunted him back.

Aphrodite was credited with many affairs and many children. She fell in love with Anchises, a young cousin of Priam, King of Troy. The result of their liaison was Aeneas, whom she guided out of the burning city of Troy and on his route to Italy. The Romans, who claimed their descent from Aeneas, had much more to say about this particular story than did the Greeks, so we will return to Aeneas later.

Aphrodite's husband was the homely but highly skilled Hephaestus, god of the fire and the forge. Some legends say this marriage was a punishment Aphrodite received for making the gods take part in so many undignified amours. This may have been fit punishment for her, but it was often rather hard on him.

Although married to Hephaestus, Aphrodite bore Eros [9] to Ares, the war god, and Homer relates in the *Odyssey* how Hephaestus, informed of their affair by the all-seeing and gossipy Helios, made a hunting net of either gold or bronze. Whatever its material, it was gossamer fine and quite unbreakable. When he had snared the lovers in it, he hung them up for all Olympus to see.

The goddesses stared in disgust, and the gods in envy of Ares.

Despite her indisputable transgressions, Aphrodite, like the other gods, was worshipped in her magnificence. The *Homeric Hymn to Aphrodite* says, "I sing praise to stately and beautiful Aphrodite, crowned in gold, who holds the ramparts of sea-girt Cyprus ... all the gods gape in amazement at the glory of violet-crowned Cytherea." Empedocles gets right to the heart of the matter: "Do you not see how mighty is the goddess Aphrodite? She sows and gives that love from which all we upon this earth are born."

9. B. Roman Venus

Evidently originating in Ardea and Lavinium in central Italy, the Roman Venus began as a nature goddess associated with the arrival of spring and as grand patroness of gardens and vineyards. Since she was also in charge of love and beauty, she was, as might have been expected, the bringer of joy to gods and humans. As we have learned to expect in Rome, Venus had several titles. As Venus Genetrix, she was worshiped as the mother of the hero Aeneas, the founder of the Roman people; as Venus Felix, she was the bringer of good fortune; as Venus Victrix, the bringer of victory; and as Venus Verticordia, the protector (of all things!) of feminine chastity.

She had numerous practical and homely duties and titles that would never have suited Greek Aphrodite. In 390 BCE the Romans were so soundly beaten at the river Allia by invading Gauls that they rushed back into the city without even closing the gates, and didn't stop running until they reached the fortified citadel on the Capitoline Hill. Here they were besieged by the Gauls, and things got so tough that Roman women gave their hair for bowstrings. Later, when the trouble was over, this sacrifice was commemorated by a dedication to Venus Calva – that is, Venus the Bald. (Servius, *Ad Aenean, I, 720)* As Rome remained standing rather than turning into a smoldering ruin, Venus evidently accepted this in the spirit in which it was meant and chose not to turn mifty about it. After all, for many years she had been accepting tributes in the small round temple of Venus Cloacina – Venus of the Sewer, which will be discussed in the Temple section.

Many stories told of Venus, as is the case with the other gods, are those told of her Greek counterpart. However, the poet Vergil in his *Aeneid* added several of his own, concerned, as might be expected, with her struggles to protect her son Aeneas from the machinations of Juno, who hated all Trojans, evidently because she had never forgotten that apple business, and who had a special prejudice against any offspring of Venus, who had been responsible for so many of Jupiter's failings. The Fates had decreed that Aeneas would escape the destruction of Troy to be the ancestor of Rome, and the Fates, as the gods sometimes learned to their cost, always had their way. Juno, however, who was not only cow-eyed but also bull-headed, thought there must be an exception to every rule. After Aeneas had stravaged about the Mediterranean for years trying to find out where he was going (the great gods who directed him to seek a new home were a bit stingy with directions), his little Penates (gods specific to a household or place about whom we will talk later) told him he was supposed to go to

Italy. After several misstarts it looked as though he was about to get there when Juno bribed Aeolus, King of the Winds, to stir up a stupendous storm and shipwreck him on the coast of Africa, entirely too close to her city of Carthage, which was ruled by a young, beautiful widow named Dido. Venus, who had a fair idea of what Juno was trying to accomplish, disguised herself as a huntress and met Aeneas as he set out down to coast trying to get his bearings and filled him in on the scene and dramatis personae of the soap opera in which he would shortly be participating. She thoughtfully concealed him and his companion Achates in a cloud of mist so that they could drift into Carthage and spy out the land before they were discovered. The Carthaginians and their queen did not notice this odd meteorological phenomenon; perhaps because they were too busy greeting some of Aeneas' men who had gotten separated from him in the storm. Just as everyone was saying, "Wish Aeneas was here", Venus dissolved the cloud, after sprucing him up a bit. Dido was suitably impressed, but just to be on the safe side Venus sent her mischievous little archer son Cupid, disguised as Aeneas' son Iulus, to the banquet the queen gave for the strangers. Needless to say, Dido never had a chance, and she not only protected Aeneas during his stay in Carthage, but committed suicide when he left for Italy. Venus, who firmly believed in the old saw about the necessity of breaking a few eggs to make an omelet, shrugged and moved on to sweet-talk various gods into helping her defend Aeneas and confound his enemies in Italy. She used all her winsome beauty and persuasiveness on the gods, and all her clever ruses on the goddesses, to achieve these ends.

According to Vergil, the Romans had excellent reasons to call her the Mother of Rome.

10. A. Ares, God of War

As there was no special god of evil in the Greek pantheon, each of the gods had a share in mischief-making, and none did a better job of it than Ares. He was tall, handsome and athletic, but also aggressive and blood-thirsty, and he liked to exercise his prowess in that most destructive of games, war. Thus it is not amazing that neither his father Zeus nor his mother Hera was especially fond of him and that his company was seldom sought in social circles, divine or human. In spite of this, an ancient Homeric hymn describes him as dancing among the other immortals to Apollo's kithara. (*Homeric Hymn 3 to Pythian Apollo, 190*)

Ares was the favored lover of Aphrodite (with whom he shared a total disregard for the opinions and rights of others, such as her husband

Hephaestus). Perhaps their mutual attraction arose because love and war are opposites, or perhaps because they often resemble each other. However that may have been, they had several offspring, such as Deimos (Fear), Phobos (Terror) and the redoubtable little archer Eros/Cupid/Amor.

Strong and terrible he might be, but Ares was not invulnerable. He made the mistake of diving headlong into the Trojan War to aid his lover Aphrodite. Aphrodite was trying to defend her son Aeneas, whom Diomedes was about to keep from ever founding Rome, or doing anything else *(Iliad 5.355)*. Diomedes wounded the goddess (a fact that he would live to regret) and she dropped Aeneas. With his horses, Flame and Terror, pulling his war chariot, Ares charged into the fray, throwing his spear and protecting Aeneas with his shield. While Aphrodite made her escape to Mount Olympus to tend her wounds, Pallas Athena, still testy over that apple business, deflected Ares' spear and threw an able-bodied boulder at him, which knocked him senseless. When he retreated to Mount Olympus his father, Zeus, commanded Paieon the all-healer to cure his wound, but said, "To me you are most hateful of all the gods of Olympus"*(Iliad 5.889)*.

Because of his prowess, he was worshipped throughout Greece, and great Greek warriors were often said to be his sons. Honored especially by warriors, he was one of the first divinities worshipped in Athens, being associated with Theseus' defeat of the Amazons.

Like any good father, Ares tried to defend his children, but did not always find it easy to do. When Halirrhothius, a son of Poseidon, tried to violate Ares' daughter Alcippe, Ares killed him. At Poseidon's insistence, Ares was tried on the Areopagus (Hill of Ares) in Athens before the twelve gods, but was acquitted. (The Areopagus became the great court of Athens, especially for homicides, and Ares reputedly was the first to be tried for murder there). When his son Kyknos was killed by Heracles *(Theogony 421)*, Ares was unable to avenge the death because Zeus would not permit his least favorite son, Ares, to harm Heracles, his favorite son.

Destructive and cruel wife-snatcher though he was, Ares, like the other Olympians, received great honor and many fervent prayers, though most of them carry a rider indicative of some wariness on the part of the devotees. For example, as *Homeric Hymn 8 to Ares* carols, "Strong Ares, golden-helmed charioteer, Savior of cities...Help me drive away cowardice," it continues, "but restrain the fury that drives me to bloody strife."

Orphic Hymn 65 to Ares [10] is even more outspoken as it pleads, "Great-souled, invincible Ares, whose mighty power can shake down the strongest walls, you who delight in blood and arms, stop the destructive strife and yield to Aphrodite."

10. B. Roman Mars

Mars, the son of Jupiter and Juno, was one of the most prominent Roman gods. In early Roman history Mars was a god of spring, growth in nature, fertility, and the protector of cattle. He is also mentioned as a chthonic god, which may explain why he became a god of death and finally a god of war. His sacred animals are the wolf and the woodpecker (which may be a noisy bird, but is more attractive than Ares' vulture). He is accompanied by Fuga and Timor, the personifications of flight and fear. He is portrayed as a warrior in full battle armor, wearing a crested helmet and bearing a shield. The old Roman god Quirinus, who seems to have started out in charge of war, was worshipped separately but often identified either with Mars or with Romulus, son of Mars and the legendary founder of Rome.

And thereby hangs a tale. In Alba Longa, the small city that would be the precursor of Rome, Good King Numitor had a Wicked Brother, Amulius. Amulius drove his brother (who seems to have been as weak as he was good) from the city and took the throne. Carefully considering the safety of his own precious skin, Amulius then arranged a sad accident for his nephew, the son of Numitor, and forced his niece Rhea Silvia to become a Vestal Virgin (emphasis on the last word). Mars, who admired Rhea Silvia and had great faith in his ability to talk around his aunt Vesta, took the Vestal to wife. The next thing Amulius knew he had twin grand-nephews, Romulus and Remus. They survived Uncle Amulius' delicate attentions, which included throwing them in the River Tiber in a leaky basket. (A she-wolf, no doubt conscious of her position as Animal Companion of Mars, dutifully fished them out of the swollen stream). True sons of Mars, when they grew up they restored the throne to Numitor, and then, finding life in their grandfather's city rather constricting, went a few miles away and founded Rome. In the course of this founding a quarrel sprang up, and Romulus killed Remus. From this story the Romans called themselves 'the sons of Mars' and paid him great homage.

11. A. Hermes, Messenger God

The *Homeric Hymn to Hermes* says that on Mt. Cyllene in Arcadia Maia bore a son, a cunning robber, a cattle driver, a bringer of dreams, a watcher by night, a thief at the gates, one who would do awesome deeds among the deathless gods. (*Homeric Hymn 4*)

Maia placed the infant in his cradle, but Hermes, who had no intention of spending his natal day in such a dull place, escaped and went out looking for amusement. Putting his divine attribute of speed to good use, he ran to Thessaly, where his brother Apollo had the Golden Oxen of the Sun grazing. Like any baby, he had a taste for pretty things, so he helped himself to a number of the graceful creatures and concealed them in a cave near Pylos. While he was watching his stolen herd, he discovered a tortoise in the cave, and killed it. Using one of the cow's intestines (evidently he had indulged in a bit of grilled steak) and the tortoise's shell, he made the first lyre. (Some say he used a sheep's intestines, but when our baby robber had time to find and finish off a sheep is a problem). Apollo complained to Maia that her son had stolen his cattle, but Hermes had already curled himself up his baby blankets, carefully concealing his new lyre under the covers. Maia refused to believe Apollo's story, and the infant prodigy Hermes, who added speech to his unusual early accomplishments, asked what cows might be. When the furious Apollo took the whole affair to Mt. Olympus, Zeus showed a tendency to side with Apollo. Hermes then began to play music on the lyre he had invented. Apollo, the god of music, fell in love with the instrument and offered to exchange the cattle for the lyre. So Hermes was off the hook and onto a running start in his divine specialties.

With his amazing speed, it was no surprise that Hermes was made the messenger of the gods. Trade was another of his specialties, so he was dear to merchants. Thieves also prayed to him, and although the cynical say that the merchants behaved so much like thieves that he got mixed up with both of them, his attribute of speed and his own activities probably had more to do with this.

In his role as the messengers of the gods, and especially as conductor of the souls of the dead to the world below (which duty gave him the dismal title of "Psychopompos -- "conductor of the soul") Hermes carried the caduceus, which was given him by Apollo in exchange for yet another musical instrument, the pipes. The caduceus was a magic wand that exercised influence over the living and the dead, and bestowed wealth and prosperity. In its oldest form it was a rod ending in two prongs twined into a knot (probably an olive branch with two shoots, adorned with ribbons or garlands), for which, later, two serpents, with heads meeting at the top, were substituted. The poets explained the change with a story of Hermes finding two serpents thus knotted together while fighting; when he separated them with his wand, crowned by the serpents, it became the symbol of the settlement of quarrels. Hermes' well-known attire was completed by Zeus when he appointed his sneaky son as herald, or messenger of the gods. For his new appointment, Zeus outfitted him with his well-known flat-crowned winged hat, his sandals with wings, and evidently as a final touch added the wings to the caduceus. Zeus smiled on his newly promoted son, but warned him that in the future he must respect property rights, refrain from telling outright lies, and safeguard travelers and commerce. (Graves, *17*) Hermes promised, smoothly and a little too quickly, to do all this.

In addition to a career in larceny grand and not so grand, Hermes, who evidently evolved from a pre-Hellenic fertility cult (Graves, *17*) had a love life which staggers the imagination. We shall blushingly take a look at only a few of the foremost of his offspring.

While tending curly-fleeced sheep in the service of a mortal man, Hermes wed the daughter of Dryopos, and she bore to him a son who from his birth was unusual, having goat's feet and two horns - a noisy, merry, laughing child. His nurse took one look at his leering face and full beard and fled. Then Hermes took him in his arms with a glad heart." (*Homeric Hymn 19 to Pan*). This remarkable offspring was the great goat-god Pan, who became the deity of herdsmen and the companion of nymphs and satyrs, of whom he was chief. He danced and played upon the Pan pipes, or Syrinx, a musical instrument so named because it had been made from reeds which had once been a maiden of that name who had fled from Pan's wooing and prayed to be turned into a bed of reeds. When she got her wish, Pan fashioned his pipes from the reeds.

A very important but confusing offspring of Hermes was a daughter borne to him by Daeira, an underworld goddess (her name also appears as a title of Persephone) who in most tales was a daughter of Oceanus who evidently represented some source of fresh-water like her brother-rivers and sister-clouds. Therefore she was probably portrayed in the Eleusinian Mysteries as the goddess of grain-nourishing groundwater which Hermes (her consort) brought up from the underworld every spring in the company of Persephone. (Pausanias *1.38)* Some say her name is probably a title for Hecate or Persephone, and that Eleusis was not a daughter but a son. Whatever the facts about her mother and her gender may have been, Eleusis, the Patron-Goddess of the Eleusinian Mysteries and the goddess of the town of Eleusis, was one of the many attendants of Demeter.

Strangest of all Hermes' children is the son of Hermes and Aphrodite, Hermaphroditos. Hermaphroditos was born of Hermes and Aphrodite and he received a name that is a combination of those of both his parents. He combined their physical aspects as well. Some said that he was born with a physical body that was a combination of that of a man and that of a woman, in that he has a body that is beautiful and delicate like that of a woman, but has the masculine quality and vigor of a man. But there are some who declare that such creatures of two sexes are monstrosities, and coming rarely into the world as they do they have the quality of presaging the future, sometimes for evil and sometimes for good. (Diodorus Siculus 4.6.5)

The Roman poet Ovid, who sees the romantic in every situation, however fantastic, says that Hermaphroditos had the bad luck to take a swim in the pool of Salmacis, where a nymph of the same name lived. When he refused her love, she clung to him and prayed to whatever mischievous gods might be listening that the two of them would be joined forever. When Hermaphroditos emerged from the pool, he had the characteristics of both a man and a woman.

In a nasty little revenge venture he prayed to his powerful parents that all men who swam in this accursed pool should be so served. (Ovid, *Metamorphoses 4.285*) (If the men of the area were unkempt and somewhat smelly, who can blame them? Bathing in this pool, or any pool, may have seemed too great a risk to take.)

As in the case of the other gods, where Hermes found the time for all this dallying is a mystery. He had a full schedule caring for the travelers who insisted on globe-trotting, guiding souls to Hades, keeping merchants on their toes, and carrying Zeus' messages all over the universe (not to mention dealing with the petitions no doubt directed to him by various and sundry merchants and thieves).

All this notwithstanding, Hermes, the beautiful wing-sandaled thief, had his good side. *Homeric Hymn 18* calls him the "luck-bringing messenger of the deathless gods, the giver of grace and good things." He is linked with the gentle Hestia as one who is kind to poor mortals. "And you, slayer of Argus, Son of Zeus and Maia, messenger of the blessed gods, bearer of the golden rod, giver of good, be favorable and help us, you and Hestia, the worshipful and dear. Come and dwell in this glorious house in friendship together; for you two, well knowing the noble actions of men, aid their wisdom and their strength (*Homeric Hymn 29*).

11. B. Roman Mercury

Mercury, son of Jupiter and Maia, was the Roman god of trade, profit and commerce; his name is possibly derived from the Latin **merx** or **mercator**, a merchant. Merchants prayed to this overseer of trade and profit in order to get good business. Originally the deity of traders in corn (by which term the Romans meant virtually any seed crop with a hard surface), he became the guardian of travelers and the messenger of the gods. Of course, the Romans had to give him at least one extra name, so he is known also as Alipes ("winged foot"). Strangely enough, the sacred animal of this handsome, quick-footed thief was the chicken, and he is sometimes depicted with one. He resembled not only the Greek god Hermes but also the Etruscan Turms. Like Hermes, he is dressed in a wide cloak, wearing **talaria** (winged sandals), and **petasus** (winged hat) and carrying the caduceus (the staff with two intertwined snakes which the Romans said to have power over sleeping, waking, and dreams). He also carries a purse or moneybag (a symbol of his connection with commerce). Vergil describes Mercury when as messenger of the gods he was preparing to take Aeneas a pretty stiff message from Jupiter concerning his dalliance with Queen Dido in Carthage. (Not that Jupiter had any objection to dalliance, as his own career abundantly proves. He just wanted Aeneas to get on to Italy and found Rome, as Venus was pestering the life out of the chief god about it. Besides, as the moment Aeneas wasn't presenting a very good example of *pietas,* which was destined to become the chief Roman virtue.[11] But we must get back to Mercury). First he donned his golden, winged sandals, then took his caduceus, with which Vergil says he summoned souls from Orcus, sent others to Tartarus, lulled men to sleep or wakened them, and opened the eyes of the dead. (*Aeneid IV, 239-244*). Mercury, Vergil says, is "golden-haired and magnificent in his youth" (*Aeneid IV, 559*), splitting the winds with his passage, then hovering on splendid wings above the earth, before he plunges down in awesome flight. (*Aeneid IV, 245, 255-57*). He promptly appears in all his splendor before the shocked Aeneas, to whom he gives a terse and effective message about immediate departure for Italy.

12. A. Hephaestus, God of Fire and Forge

Hephaestus, the lame god of fire and the god of volcanoes, was very early associated with the blacksmith's fire. He became the patron of all craftsmen, especially those working with metals, and was worshiped in manufacturing centers. Although he was the son of Zeus and Hera or, in some accounts, of Hera alone, Hephaestus, even more than Hestia, found himself ill at ease on Mount Olympus. Not only did he tend, like her, to simple straightforward behavior rather than the Byzantine plots of other Olympians, but he wasn't even good-looking. In stark contrast to the golden athletic perfection of his Olympian siblings, Hephaestus was generally represented as a sturdy and muscular man with a thick neck and hairy chest who, because of a shortened, lame leg and club foot, supported himself with the aid of a crutch. This humble hard-working god most often was shown dressed in a ragged sleeveless tunic and woolen hat, an ensemble in which no other Olympian deity would ever have appeared.

Some legends state that he was so ugly and unappealing at birth that Hera, his mother, threw him from the walls of Olympus into the sea, where he was rescued by the sea-nymph Thetis. After Hera saw the lovely jewelry he made for Thetis at his forge, she insisted that he return to Mount Olympus to ply his trade. Never in her divine arrogance having paused to consider whether those she had injured in the past might be less than pleased with her autocratic commands, Hera delighted in a very beautiful golden throne that Hephaestus made for her. When she sat on it, however, it entrapped her, making her a prisoner. The Olympian gods pleaded with Hephaestus to release Hera, but he refused. Zeus, to no one's surprise, resorted to trickery. He sent Dionysus, the god of wine, to offer his brother some of his most outstanding vintage. Hephaestus received his initiation into the joys of the grape, and, rendered affable and obliging by his potations, then mounted a donkey and, accompanied by Dionysus, rode back to Mount Olympus. Some say that before releasing Hera however, Hephaestus insisted upon being given the beautiful Aphrodite as his bride, a reward that often proved to be a punishment in itself.

However rocky his relationship with his mother might have been, Hephaestus argued for her when Zeus hung her in chains for rebelling against him. Not only did this intervention bring no help to Hera, it bought Hephaestus another swift descent from Olympus. This time Zeus threw him over the wall, and he landed on hard earth, breaking both his legs. He was eventually pardoned, but he was lame and, perhaps understandably, ill-tempered. As we have seen in previous stories, his temper was scarcely improved by his marriage to Aphrodite, who had not one trace of fidelity or constancy in her dazzling body.

As divine craftsman-in-chief, Hephaestus manufactured wonderful articles from many materials, though his favorite was metal. His masterpieces included the palaces of gods atop Mount Olympus and the thunderbolts and scepter of Zeus as well as the weapons and accoutrements of most of the other gods, but he spent little time on Mount Olympus unless he was actually working there. He was associated throughout Greek history with several volcanoes, especially Mount Etna in Sicily, and he preferred to ply his craft under his favorite volcano with help from the Cyclopes, who were his workmen and assistants. There he made the chariot, or according to some, the golden cup or goblet, which the sun god Helios rode across the sky, Athena's shield or aegis, and the arrows of Eros, the god of love. He also made accoutrements for heroes, among which were various articles for Heracles and the wonderful armor of Achilles which Homer takes great pains and many lines of the *Iliad* to discuss. To help him and his Cyclopes with all these commissions Hephaestus made a set of golden maidens who moved and did his bidding.

Prometheus stole the fire that he gave to man from Hephaestus' forge, and, perhaps because of this, we have seen that Zeus commanded Hephaestus to create the first woman, Pandora, who, according to that old misogynist Hesiod, brought all sorts of catastrophes on mankind.

It was also Hephaestus who, following Zeus' instructions, reluctantly chained Prometheus to the rock in Mount Caucasus with the help of Cratos (Power) and Bia (Violence):

"Against my will, no less than yours, I must rivet you with brazen bonds ... Such is the prize you have gained for your championship of man." ([Hephaestus to Promethus] Aeschylus, *Prometheus Bound* 20]

Hephaestus: Oh handicraft that I hate so much!

Cratos: Why hate it? Your craft is not to blame for these present troubles.

Hephaestus: Nevertheless, I wish it had fallen to another's lot! (Aeschylus, *Prometheus Bound* 45)

Hephaestus was one of the very small minority of deities who were for the most part kind and gentle; thus he was beloved on earth. He and Athena were especially important to cities, where Hephaestus protected the smiths and Athena the weavers. The people revered and paid homage to these important deities. "Sing, clear-voiced Muses, of Hephaestus renowned for inventions. With bright-eyed Athene he taught glorious arts throughout the world to men, who before he came dwelled in mountain caves like wild beasts. Now that they have learned crafts through Hephaestus the brilliant worker, they live a peaceful easy life in their own houses the whole year round." (*Homeric Hymn 11. 1-7*)

Vulcan, God of Fire and Forge

12. B. Roman Vulcan

The Roman fire god Vulcan, also called Mulciber, was very old. His Volcanal altar was one of the most ancient religious centers of Rome, and his festival, the Vulcanalia, dated back to the ancient Roman kingdom. He was the son of Jupiter and Juno, two of the Capitoline Triad, and the husband of Venus. Although he was the divine craftsman who made art, arms and armor for gods and heroes, Vulcan seems to have originated as a god of volcanoes; thus the Romans were never as comfortable with him as the Greeks were with Hephaestus. With a wary eye on the destructive nature of his firepower, the Romans tended to build his temples outside of town. Yet in the pious hope of obtaining his protection in averting fires, they dedicated numerous shrines or altars to him in places where fires were most feared, such as areas near volcanoes and where grain was stored, especially at the port of Ostia. He was the protector of smiths, and was normally depicted as a bearded man, dressed as a worker and carrying the utensils of a smith.

The Romans said that his fiery workshop was inside the volcano Mount Etna on the island of Sicily. There he with his helpers, the one-eyed Cyclopes and the golden maidens he had crafted, created his magnificent works.

He was linked with several primary goddesses including Maia (as another Earth Mother), and Vesta, in her role as earth goddess. In addition to his ill-starred marriage to Venus, he had short-term relationships with other females. His offspring seemed generally to have been monstrous, such as the giant Cacus. Cacus, who had been half man and half something too monstrous to be described, had belched forth fire that he got from his father and proved to be a real nuisance to the very early people of central Italy until he made the fatal mistake of rustling some cattle belonging to Heracles. (Vergil, *Aeneid, VIII, 185-267*).

Vulcan was sad about the death of his son and often displeased with the activities of Venus, but, influenced by a combination of his sympathy for a harassed warrior and his desire to please his beautiful wife, who could be incredibly winsome when she chose, he outdid his usual superb craftsmanship when Aeneas went into his life-or-death struggle with the forces of the Italian warrior chief Turnus. Vergil devotes more than 120 lines in Book VIII of the *Aeneid* to the helmet gushing flame, the sword-blade edged with fate, and the blood-red bronze breastplate that Vulcan made for Aeneas, before waxing truly rhapsodic about the giant shield on which he depicted the future history of Rome (*Aeneid, VIII, ll. 608-731*).

Chapter IV - The Great Earth Gods

1. A. Demeter, Goddess of Agriculture

In Greek mythology Demeter, the daughter of Cronus and Rhea and sister of Zeus, was goddess of agriculture and civilized life. With such a pedigree, one might expect her to rank among the twelve great Olympians, but neither Homer nor Hesiod places her there; she is simply the great, good, and sorrowing grain goddess. (After all, being a female associated with the productivity of the soil, she was about as chthonian as one could get). Her name has been explained as (1) grain-mother, from the Cretan form of wheat, barley, or (2) earth-mother in the Doric form. Her influence, however, was not limited to grain, but extended to livestock and fruits of the earth in general with the curious exception of the bean, the use of which was forbidden at Eleusis, and for the protection of which a special patron was invented.[12] Her attributes are what might be expected: ears of corn, the poppy, the mystic basket (*calathus*) filled with flowers, corn and fruit of all kinds, the pomegranate being especially common. (Again, these are not the adornments of an Olympian female divinity, being lamentably short on baubles, bangles and beads). Of animals, the cow and the pig are her favorites, the latter because of its productivity and the cathartic properties of its blood. (Exactly what were the cathartic properties of pig's blood is a study we prefer to leave to someone else; in fact, anyone else). Sacred to her, in addition to a grand array of livestock and agricultural products, are the poppy, asphodel, narcissus (which Persephone was gathering when carried off by Hades) and the crane, which is an indicator of the weather. As a chthonian divinity, she is often accompanied by a snake.

The rituals concerning her, among the most important in Greece, were closely linked with her children, one of whom is her son Plutus. Hesiod has this to say about this offspring: "Demeter, the shining goddess, was joined in sweet love with the hero Iasion in a field in the fertile countryside of Crete, and brought forth Plutus, a kindly god who moves across both land and the wide sea; he bestows great wealth on those who find him." (*Theogony 969-974*) Homer adds a bit about Demeter's short-term consort: "So when Demeter fell in love with Iasion, and yielded to him in a thrice-ploughed fallow field, Zeus soon heard of it and killed Iasion with his thunderbolts." (*Odyssey V, 125*) (If any one should wonder just who this short-lived lover of the goddess may be, Apollodorus *[Apollodorus 3.138,]* says that this Iasion, lover of the great goddess, is the son of Zeus and Electra, but this is only one of six versions of Iasion's ancestry.) Both Homer and Hesiod place Demeter's brief romance in Crete.

Whatever the details may have been, the result was Plutus, the Greek god who personifies wealth. His attributes are a cornucopia and a basket filled with ears of corn. According to an extant but little regarded comedy of Aristophanes, the *Plutus*, Zeus blinded him because he distributed his gifts without regard to merit (why Zeus took exception to this behavior in him, when most of the gods were often guilty of the same, is never explained). At Thebes, there was a statue of Fortune holding the child Plutus in her arms; at Athens he was similarly represented in the arms of Peace; at Thespiae he was represented standing beside Athena the Worker. Elsewhere he was represented as a boy with a cornucopia.

Both Plutus and his father Iasion play their parts in Demeter's great ritual, the Eleusinian Mysteries, but they had poor press agents and were little known outside the Mysteries. Even there, the central feature of her cult, and the cause of her eternal sorrow, was the story of her daughter Persephone, We have already seen that Persephone, daughter of Demeter and Zeus, was carried off by Hades to the underworld. Demeter, wild with grief and showing the typical divine disregard for consequences, gave no fruitfulness to the earth, which promptly grew barren. To make matters worse, on finding a portion of Persephone's girdle, Demeter cursed the earth and the green plants all withered. Wandering across the wasteland she had created, ever searching for her daughter, Demeter came to Eleusis. Disguised as old woman named Deo, she arrived at the house of Celeus at Eleusis, where she was hospitably received. The family invited the goddess to stay for dinner (which, with the earth in this state, was likely to be skimpy) and told her about their son and brother who was dying. Demeter gathered poppies, (we can only wonder where she had left any growing) and upon seeing the child, kissed him on the lips to restore his vitality and secretly placed poppy juice in his milk. Later that night, intending to give him immortality, she re-formed him, and started to throw him into the fire for purification. The boy's mother, understandably disturbed by the thought of her son becoming an ember, intervened. Demeter revealed her radiant form to the mother, and admonished her for being so protective.

The son missed immortality (which some mortals, such as the Cumaean Sibyl, could tell him had its drawbacks), but grew up to teach cultivation of the soil.

Demeter continued to search for her daughter until finally the sun-god Helios (or in some versions the spring Arethusa) feeling that enough was enough, finally told her the truth: that Persephone had become Queen of the Underworld, and the wife of Pluto. Demeter appealed to Zeus for her return, and Zeus, realizing that something must be done if man or beast was to survive, agreed on the condition that Persephone had not taken any food in the underworld. Hades, who had had a sneaking suspicion that affairs were coming to a crisis, had offered her a pomegranate, known as the food of the dead, so she would be forced to return to him. So, as Persephone had accepted a pomegranate from Pluto, and tasted the pulp of its seed, she must reside with her mother no more than half of each year. The remaining time she must spend with her husband in Hades. Demeter restored fruitfulness to the earth, but only for such time as she had her daughter with her.

In Greek art, Demeter is made to resemble Hera, only more matronly and of milder expression; her form is broader and fuller. She is sometimes riding in a chariot drawn by horses or dragons, sometimes walking, sometimes seated upon a throne, alone or with her daughter. The Demeter of Cnidus in the British Museum, of the school of Praxiteles, apparently shows her mourning f or the loss of her daughter.

The Greeks loved and venerated her as giving and loving, not fierce. "Demeter Eleusinia, universal mother, Deo renowned and venerable ... great nurse, all-giving, blessed and divine, lover of peace and nourisher of the corn. Beautiful queen, nurse of all mortals; glorious, bright, and kind, bright and holy in nature. To you belong all the flowers, and fruits lovely and green. Bright Goddess, come, bring summer's rich growth, peace, harmony and health, and with them the wealth we need." — *Orphic Hymn 40 to Demeter*

1. B. Roman Ceres

Ceres was the ancient Italian goddess of agriculture; she was also chief representative of the love a mother bears for her child. Her cult was closely connected with that of Tellus, the Goddess Earth. *"Let Tellus, fertile in fruits and herds, present Ceres with a crown of wheat stalks; let the healthy waters and breezes of Jupiter nourish the offspring."* (Horace, *Carmen Saeculare* 29-32). The Romans gave Ceres credit for the development of agriculture, saying that she was first to gather the wild corn and show men how to prepare it, preserve it, and sow it. Fully aware that replacing the hunter's life with agriculture would lead to people to a settled life in close proximity to each other, she also introduced laws, so that settlement of their inevitable squabbles would possess some justice and fairness. "Ceres was the first to turn the sod with the hooked plow-share; she first gave laws. All things are the gift of Ceres; she must be the subject of my song." (Ovid *Metamorphoses V, 341-344*)

Unlike Demeter, who never made the list of the Twelve Great Olympians, Ceres was a member of the Dii Consentes. In later mythology, she was the daughter of Saturn and Rhea, the consort and sister of Jupiter (Romans, like most mythologists, never worried about consistency, or what Juno's reaction to this situation must have been), and mother of Proserpina (Persephone). Ceres is portrayed with a scepter, a basket with flowers or fruits, and a garland made of ears of corn.

Curiously enough, in spite of her presence among the Dii Consentes, Roman Ceres was specifically the goddess of the plebs, or common people. Various reasons for this have been suggested. One of the more convincing states that her ancient associations with agriculture and fertility made her a commonly worshiped deity among Latin farmers. The patricians, being a jealous lot, are even said to have imported the worship of the Magna Mater, Cybele of Asia Minor, so that they might have a goddess similar to Ceres for their own. (After all, according to Vergil [*Aeneid Book IX*] Cybele had given her holy forest in Asia Minor to build Aeneas' fleet for his journey to Italy, and generally assisted in the founding of Rome.)

Thus there came to be a triad on the Aventine hill more in tune with the common people that the lofty Capitoline Triad. Slowly the Aventine Triad of Ceres, the grain goddess, Liber, the god of masculinity and wine, and Libera, Liber's feminine counterpart, became identified with Demeter, Dionysus and Persephone, and the story of the lost daughter became part of their story. Thus it was said that Hades kidnapped Ceres' daughter Proserpina, and Ceres was so grief-stricken that she refused to allow anything on Earth to be beautiful or fruitful while Proserpina was underground, only allowing summer and harvest-time when she had her daughter with her.

1. C. Cybele

Cybele, known as the Magna Mater, was one of the ubiquitous forms of the Earth Mother. Roughly equivalent to Rhea, or sometimes Gaia, in

Greece she was evidently brought to Rome by the patricians specifically to be a rival to Ceres, who was seen as belonging to the plebeians. In her original home in Phrygia, she presided over mountains and fortresses, and her crown was in the form of a city wall. According to Ovid, it was Cybele who transformed the heroine Atalanta and her consort Hippomenes into lions because they had defiled her temple, and ever after they drew her chariot.

As Cybele the Magna Mater was the Goddess of nature and fertility, her rituals were often orgiastic, but this does not seem to have led the Roman Senate to ban them, as we shall see they did the festivals of Bacchus. After all, she had been imported by the patrician, or senatorial, class, and they weren't about to admit that they had made this, or any other, mistake.

2. A. Dionysus, God of Wine

We have already discussed the birth of Dionysus the wine god as given by Hesiod (*Theogony, 900-942*). We have seen that Hera's jealousy led the unfortunate Semele to ask Zeus for a fatal favor, and that Dionysus was only saved from being consumed in the resulting conflagration along with his mother by the quick action of Zeus, who snatched the unborn baby and hid it in his thigh. "The Father of men and gods brought you to birth concealed from mankind and from Hera, at Nysa, a great mountain in far off Phoenice richly rich with forests, near the streams of Aegyptus. (*Homeric Hymn to Dionysus 11, 7-9*) Be kind, O Insewn god, Inspirer of frenzied women! We sing of you as we begin and as we end a strain, and no one who forgets you can remember holy song. And so, farewell, Dionysus, the Insewn, with your mother Semele whom men call Thyone. (*Homeric Hymn to Dionysus 11, 17-21*)" Hera, who was never known to give up a project easily, was still jealous and arranged for the Titans to kill Dionysus. These gentle souls ripped him into to pieces, but his grandmother Rhea brought him back to life (evidently after putting him back together). After this Zeus made careful arrangements for his protection and turned him over the mountain nymphs to be raised. (At this point some researchers insert Dionysus 1 and Dionysus 2, making him separate gods before and after all this unpleasantness. For our simple survey, one is enough, and sometimes more than enough).

However much this story of his birth places him squarely in the Olympian family tree (and a typical Olympian fracas), Dionysus was not one of the Big Twelve, and the story persisted that he was not truly Greek at all, but imported. Some scholars have long suspected that Dionysus has two distinct origins, being in fact a fusion of a local Greek nature god and another more potent god imported rather late in Greek pre-history from Phrygia or Thrace. (See Dionysus 1 and Dionysus 2 above) He was certainly multi-faceted enough to have two, or more than two, prototypes. He was not only the god of wine, agriculture, and fertility of nature, but also, as the inspirer of poetry or song, the patron god of the Greek stage, in whose honor some of the finest drama the world has seen was written and staged. "Hail, child of beautiful Semele! He who forgets you can never order sweet song." (*Homeric Hymn 7: To Dionysus 58-59*). In addition to this he was very important in the mystery religions, such as those practiced at Eleusis, where he was closely associated with Demeter and Persephone. Perhaps because of his connection with wine, he represented ecstasy, escape from the humdrum world through intoxication (physical or spiritual), and initiation into secret rites typical of mystery religions.

Those dealing with classical gods were always well advised to tread warily, but Dionysus was more dangerous than most, as he had a dual nature, reflecting the powers of wine. While he could bring joy and ease from sorrow, he also inspired brutal, unthinking rage which could drive men (and women) mad.

No normal fetters could hold him or his followers. *Homeric Hymn 7* tells the story of a set of ill-fated pirates who learned this the hard way. Dionysus was evidently loitering about the seashore without the drinking vessel, ivy wreath, grape vines, and the thyrsos (a long fennel stalk wrapped with ivy leaves and topped with what appears to be a pine cone) which were his usual accoutrements. Seeing a handsome young man in a rich purple robe on the shore, the pirates seized him and took him on board their ship, dreaming of the ransom sure to be paid for a king's son. Dionysus, who among other things had a nasty sense of humor, allowed them to lead him on board and sat smiling as they tried to tie him up with ropes, which fell apart as they touched him. The helmsman of the ship cried out that this was a god, and they had best let him go and ask his pardon, but the captain was countenancing no such craven behavior. He ordered the sailors to put out to sea, but even as they did fragrant wine ran along the decks and grape vines grew from the masts. Before they had recovered from this unusual sight, Dionysus changed himself into a roaring lion and charged them. The sailors ran and gathered around the helmsman who had had the right idea in the first place. As the lion Dionysus seized the captain, however, they lost their nerve and dived into the sea. Dionysus changed them into dolphins and then rewarded the cautious helmsman richly.

According to some myths, Dionysus, more gallant than many gods, rescued the Cretan princess Ariadne after she had been abandoned by Theseus on the island of Naxos. As noted earlier, Ariadne had helped Theseus escape from the Minotaur, and, according to most of the stories, he sneakily sailed away from Naxos and left her sleeping. Dionysus rode to the rescue, probably in his chariot drawn by lions or leopards, which might have scared the poor girl into fits if he had not distracted her by presenting her with a golden crown studded with gems. Some say this gorgeous bauble had belonged to Thetis, and was a work of Hephaestus. However that may have been, the crown served as a wedding present. When Ariadne died, Dionysus took the crown and threw it up into the sky, where it remains fixed in the heavens as a constellation. (Other versions of the Ariadne myth are less cheery, saying that she hanged herself in despair or was slain by Artemis. But we have had more than enough of despair and slaying in this tome, and shall therefore stay with the 'happily ever after' version).

Dionysus is also one of the very few who were able to bring a dead person out of the underworld. He went to that dismal realm to find his mother Semele, whom he had never seen. He faced down Thanatos, the dreadful god of death, and brought her back to Mount Olympus. (We might think that for an immortal to face Thanatos was not so difficult, as he himself could not die -- at least not permanently. Getting this Grim Reaper to hand over on of his flock, however, was no simple matter).

Dionysus wished to reward King Midas for rescuing old Silenus, who had protected the youthful god and then become the most enthusiastic consumer of his wines, when the old drunkard had staggered into the hands of mischievous peasants. (Peasants, when not fully occupied with being downtrodden, sometimes compensated for their woes by picking on others). As a result of Silenus' rescue Dionysos granted the king one wish. King Midas chose, despite the advice of Dionysos, the ability to change everything he touched into gold. He had great fun beautifying his surroundings until lunchtime came, when his food underwent the metallic makeover. He then begged Dionysos to relieve him from his folly, and the god, laughing, told him to bathe in the river Pactolus. Midas was relieved of his inconvenient gift, and the river still sparkles with gold.

These stories of his kindness, however, must be matched against the stories of how Dionysus, when he moved into a new city and was resisted, destroyed those who opposed him. Euripides' play *The Bacchae*, written while the playwright was in the court of King Archelaus of Macedon, is the most famous of these. In this play we see Dionysus as very destructive and his worship very dangerous. Scholars have speculated not unreasonably that in Macedon Euripides discovered a more extreme form of the religion of Dionysus than the more civil, quiet forms in Athens. (Perhaps we should note that the name of the play indicates not Dionysus but Bacchus, which in both Greece and Rome indicated a much more unsavory character than his other face, Dionysus or Liber. We might also remember that Hera, never giving up on any object of her vengeance, drove him mad now and again).

In the play, Dionysus returns to Thebes, which is said to be his birthplace, where his cousin Pentheus is king, to punish any in Thebes who deny that he is a god. Pentheus has been enraged by the worship of Dionysus and has forbidden it, but he cannot stop the women, even his mother Agave, from rushing into the wilderness with the Maenads (women under the orgiastic spell of Dionysus, crazy with wine, wearing a fawn skins on their shoulders and carrying the thyrsos. It was said that in their madness they would rip apart and eat raw any animal they came upon). Dionysus lures Pentheus to the wilds where he is killed by the Maenads and then mutilated by Agave.

Dionysus was one of the most important gods in everyday life, not only because he was the guardian of an important crop, but also because he became associated with several key concepts. One was rebirth after death. (Here his dismemberment by the Titans and return to life is symbolically echoed in tending vines, where the vines must be pruned back sharply, and then become dormant in winter if they are to bear fruit in the spring). Another concept is the idea that under the influence of wine, one could feel possessed by a greater power. Unlike the other gods, Dionysus was within his believers, and he might make a man greater then himself and lead him to do (or to think that he could do) works he otherwise could not.

The characteristics of Dionysus, god of wine, who popularly represents emotion and chaos, were sometimes contrasted to those of Apollo, who represents harmony, order, and reason (for this pleasing literary picture the ancients glossed over that bow-bending side of Apollo). However, Greeks thought of the two qualities as complementary: the two gods are brothers, and when Apollo at winter left for Hyperborea, he would leave the Delphi Oracle to Dionysus. (When one thinks about it, the ravings of the Pythia, the Delphic priestess, sound more like the work of Dionysus than that of Apollo).

We have seen that, after Hephaestus had gotten revenge on his unloving mother Hera by imprisoning her on a golden throne, none of the Olympians could get him to return to Olympus to release her until Dionysus gave the smith God wine, and, after Hephaestus was intoxicated, took him back to Mount Olympus slumped over the back of a mule. Some say that while Hephaestus' two-edged reward for the release of Hera was the beautiful Aphrodite, Dionysus was rewarded by being made one of the Olympian Pantheon.

2. B. Roman Liber/Bacchus

The name of the Roman wine god Liber, like that of his counterpart deity Libera, is derived from the Latin word that meant "liberation". After the formation of the Aventine Triad, he absorbed the mythology of Dionysus. Liber may or may not have been the god of wine before this took place. (His feminine counterpart, as we have seen, through the identification of Ceres with Demeter wound up being equated to Persephone. Some claimed that Libera was the counterpart of Ariadne, who was a goddess or demigoddess. If so, Ariadne lost out when better tale came along).

Liber himself never seems to have been viewed as particularly dangerous or subversive, being associated with growing vines or, at the outside, fertility in general, vegetable and human. His festival was a homey affair, at which old ladies sold honey cakes in the street. As in Greece however, his Bacchus persona was another matter. The Bacchanalia, orgies in honor of Dionysus, were introduced in Rome around 200 BCE. It took only fourteen years for the Romans to decide that these infamous celebrations, notorious not only for sexuality but also for criminality, had to go. The Roman Senate forbade them in 186 BCE. As happens so often in such cases, the legislation gave the legislators a comfortable feeling of having done the right thing, but had very little effect on the festivals. A really sensational revel is hard to uproot.

Chapter V- Uniquely Roman Deities

1. Dii Consentes

We have already noted the group of twelve Gods called Dii Consentes: Iuppiter, Iuno, Minerva, Vesta, Ceres, Diana, Venus, Mars, Mercurius, Neptunus, Volcanus, and Apollo. These were so heavily influenced by the influx of first Etruscan and then Greek culture that they have been discussed along with the changes they underwent in the sections on the Olympians and the Earth Gods.

2. Dii Familiaris
2. A. Lares

The true heart of the traditional Roman religion centered upon the household or family cult of the Dii Familiaris. Chief among these were the Lar Familiaris, the genius or guardian spirit of the family, the Lares Loci, who were the guardian spirits of places such as house sites, and the Genius[13] or guardian angel of the paterfamilias, the head of the family. (This individual little fellow is not to be confused with the Lar, who represented the whole family. The genius of the paterfamilias was often represented by a man with a toga drawn over the head as in worship. In household shrines, there were two figures; a bearded man representing the genius of the father, and a woman representing the juno of the mother). The Lares were good spirits of the departed, particularly of family ancestors.

2. B. Penates

Lares were assisted by the two Dii Penates, the gods of the storeroom. The household cult was so important that it even served as the model for several practices of the state cult (e.g., there were the Lar Praestites, Penates Publici, etc. The ghost of the slain Trojan hero Hector tells Aeneas to flee the burning city and carry the Penates of Troy to a new home. When Aeneas leaves Troy, he entrusts the little gods to his father, as his own hands, having shed blood, must be purified before he can touch them. (*Aeneid, Book II*). After Aeneas has wandered over a good part of the eastern Mediterranean seeking his ancestral home, the Penates, perhaps a bit weary of being stuffed in a trunk and carted over the sea, come to him in a dream and tell him that Italy is the land he wants. (*Aeneid, Book III*)

2. C. Genius and Juno

The Genius, who was basic to Roman religion as the guardian spirit of a single man, like the Lar and the Penates advanced from household deity to state deity. References are made during the Late Roman Republic to the temple of the Genius of the Roman People. During the Empire, the Imperial cult came to be based on the household cult, now interpreted as the cult of the Genius of the Emperor, paterfamilias of the family of all the Romans. To curse or dishonor a man's Genius had always been a dire insult and a wish for his death. Christians, considering honors offered to the Genius of the Emperor idolatry, sometimes faced the ultimate penalty for their refusal to pay such respects. [18] As men had a personal Genius, women had a personal Juno

3. Janus, God of Doors

Janus was the most important of the purely Roman deities, and his name was invoked even before that of Jupiter himself. This "god of gods" was thought to be the oldest of the Roman gods, probably pre-dating the introduction of Jupiter and the Capitoline Triad, which appear to have Etruscan origins. (Considering the activities of ancient deities, it should come as no surprise that Janus was literally two-faced, having a countenance in front and one in back. Thus, he was known as Janus Geminus [twin] or Bifrons, with two faces looking in opposite directions. Even worse, in later times he was sometimes depicted as Janus Quadrifrons [the four-faced]). All doors and gates were sacred to this Roman god who could look both ways at once. He was also, suitably enough, the god of beginnings and endings. As the god of beginnings, he was very important to the Romans, because if an undertaking had an unsuccessful beginning, it would lead to failure. Thus, Janus' blessing was always sought in new undertakings, as well as at the beginning of every day, month, and year. The first month of the reconstructed year, January, is named after him. (Purists will remind us that the first month of the most ancient Roman calendar was March, and Numa Pompilius was said to have added January and perhaps February to the roster, finding that 10 months and 304 days did not fit very well with the habits of the sun, which showed no signs of changing its ways to suit the calendar). Janus was also the god who presided over the sowing of the crops, as sowing represented a beginning. Although as a purely Roman deity he has no history of scandalous doings such as the Olympians had, Janus did marry Juturna, the goddess of springs, and became the father of Fontus, the god of fountains.

Roman Janus

The ancient Mediterranean world was a teeming mass of deities in every conceivable place performing every conceivable function. As John Ruskin said, "A Greek never entered a wood without expecting to meet a god in it." (*Modern Painters*, 1856) While such expectations could be unsettling, they gave a zest and unpredictability to the classical world that our world conspicuously lacks. Somehow meeting a logging crew or a grizzly bear who wants a handout of snack food just doesn't have the same appeal.

Part II Temples and Festivals of the Gods

The hair-raising stories of classical gods and monsters fascinate us as do fairy tales. To the ancients, however, these were much more than characters whose legendary exploits could beguile those long winter nights before television. An examination of the places where they were worshiped and the festivals held in their honor can bring us a truer sense of the seriousness with which the ancients regarded their rambunctious deities and how they fitted into the lives of classical societies.

Section I. Elder Gods

1. A. Temples and Festivals of Cronus and Rhea

Although greatly outshone by their Olympian offspring, Cronus and Rhea had a modest temple in the gigantic Olympeion in Athens. There was also a festival called Kronia held to honor Cronus and to celebrate the harvest. Here he was praised as "Eternal father, mighty Titan, great sire of gods and men, filled with wisdom, pure and strong, through whom all forms of matter arise, die, and arise again, Birth Power and Root from which the world arose." – *Orphic Hymn 13 to Cronus*

The *Orphic Hymn to Rhea*, after a careful note recommending the ritual "fumigation from aromatics" to summon the deity, calls upon her as "daughter of earth and sky, whose chariot is drawn by fierce lions (this intimates that Rhea is also Cybele, whom we shall discuss later), mother of storms whose lightning shakes the fearful shield with drums and brass." It goes on to inform her, as Mother of War, that the "frenzied dance has begun," an indication that her rituals were lively, to say the least, and asks her to bring abundance and drive away disease.

We blush to admit that these hymns indicate that fertility of lands and people lies at the base of these rituals. Rituals designed to promote fertility often assumed characteristics delicacy forbids us to mention.

1. B. Temples and Festivals of Saturn

Saturn, the Roman deity who was a rough equivalent to Cronus, was honored in the Roman Forum with the oldest Roman temple recorded by the pontiffs. Curiously, it contained the National Treasury, so this ancient and agricultural deity evidently had mercenary duties. The temple had been dedicated, appropriately enough, on the official Saturnalia, December 17, and each year the woolen bonds that fettered the feet of the ivory cult statue within were loosened on that day to symbolize the liberation of the god.

We have already mentioned that this festival was one of the most important in Rome. Early in December the Roman farmer had usually finished his autumn planting and, as the winter solstice (December 25 in the Julian calendar) approached, felt like honoring Saturnus, the god of seed and sowing, with a lavish festival in hopes of an equally lavish harvest. As holidays the world over have a way of doing, as people found more and more ways to enjoy themselves during Saturnalia, it expanded. By Cicero's time the holiday lasted seven days, from December 17-23. The original day, the 17th, was given over to the Opalia, honoring Ops, the consort of Saturn, who personified abundance and the fruits of the earth. As the two deities represented the produce of the fields and orchards, so they also were thought to represent heaven and earth. It was for this reason, says Macrobius (*I.10.20*), that the festivals were celebrated at the same time, the worshippers of Ops always sitting in prayer so that they touched the earth, mother of all, while Saturn received sacrifices from celebrants with uncovered heads. The roles of master and slave were exchanged, and feasting and gift giving were the order of the day. Such an occasion offers many possibilities for amusement, so, when the prayers and offerings had been dispensed with, the celebrants got down to the fun part. Persons acquainted with filmdom's conception of a Roman holiday may find sadly disappointing the original authors' rather tame descriptions of the actual events. Gellius describes rotating dinner parties at which guessing games were played and the prize was a book (*Noctes Atticae, XVIII. 2*). Martial speaks of *Saturnalia* gifts such as umbrellas and oxtail brushes drawn by lot by party guests in his *Xenia* and *Apophoreta*. These two books were published in December and were intended to accompany or perhaps replace "guest gifts" such as the ones mentioned above. Macrobius' *Saturnalia* presents what he insists is a transcript of conversations held by a group of friends over several days during the festival before, during and after dinner. This is a potpourri of discussions antiquarian, religious, literary, philological, and medical, interspersed with jokes and a bit of gossip. The overall picture is of pleasant but hardly sensational pastimes. (The author, realizing that humankind prefers depraved and orgiastic Romans, regrets the necessity of reporting all this).

Section II. Olympians

The most spectacular of the ancient temples and festivals tended to center in Greece around the Twelve Olympians and the two great Earth Gods and in Italy around their counterparts the Dii Consentes. These major gods, (as well as some of the lesser ones) had temples scattered across the Mediterranean world, many built by the Greeks and still more built or rebuilt by the Romans. It is difficult for moderns to get an accurate picture of these edifices, numerous as they were. The early proponents of modern religions, scandalized by classical worship in general and fertility rites in particular, energetically took up destruction of such temples and shrines as earthquake, fire, flood and invading armies had spared. Therefore, one or two major ones for each god will be described here. In the first section, dealing with Zeus' temple at Olympia, drawings of the temple floor plan and detailed descriptions will be given. These will provide for readers a general idea of the architecture, stupendous size, and elaborate embellishments of such structures, as they were often variations on the established theme.

1. A. Temples of Zeus
The Temple of Zeus at Olympia

Pausanias (*Description of Greece 5.10.3*) wrote that the Temple of Zeus at Olympia (constructed between 470 and 456 BCE) was the largest temple in Greece before the construction of the Parthenon. The city of Elis, in a rush of joy at having defeated their neighbor Pisa in battle, commissioned one Libon of Elis to use the funds taken from Pisa to construct a really outstanding tribute to Zeus. Libon came up with something designed to stun all beholders -- a gigantic limestone structure in the pure Doric style, standing on a three-step foundation with a masonry ramp leading up to the center of the east facade, as Greek temples generally faced the east. After an earthquake in the fifth century BCE flattened the temple, pieces small enough to be carted off were used by enterprising scavengers, but the pieces recovered, (and those too big to be moved) give us an idea of the sheer grandiose magnitude of the temple. Each of the colossal Doric columns of the temple was constructed of several huge drums more than six feet in diameter, dwarfing an average-sized man who stands next to one. It is not surprising that these delicate pieces of masonry lie where they fell, layered atop one another like gigantic dominoes. There were six of these modest little structures on each facade and thirty-four in the entire colonnade.

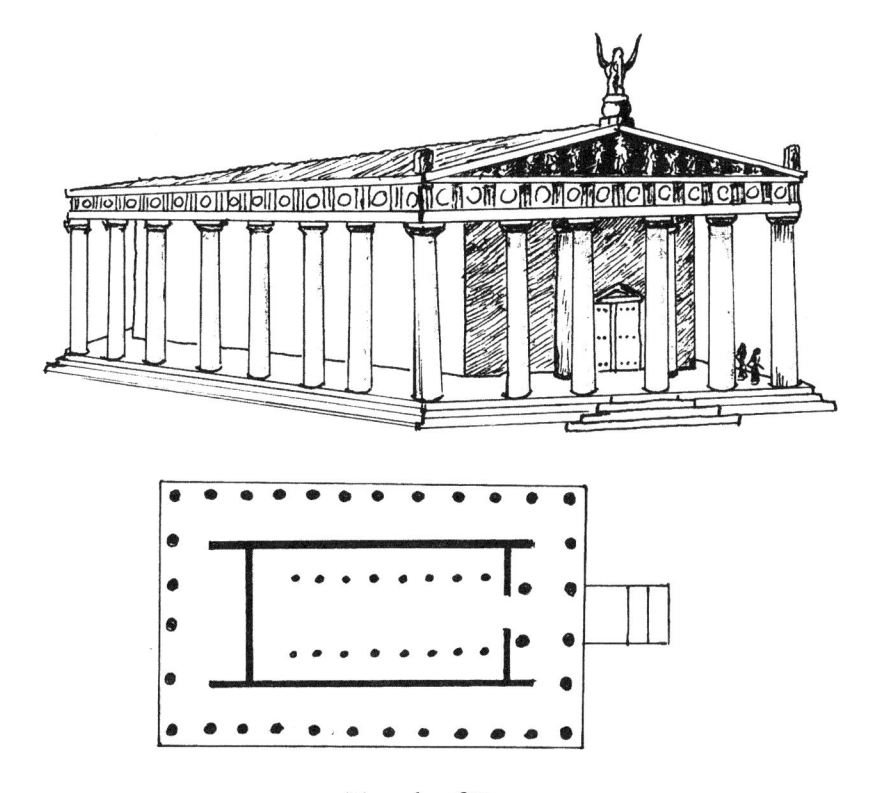

Temple of Zeus

The pediments (triangular areas supporting the roof) measured approximately 80' long by 10' tall by 3' deep. Since pediments were designed not only to support the roof, but also to give artistic visual lessons in mythology, these giant economy size ones created two problems; the first of which was to support the weight of the sculptures which adorned them, and the second to produce a unified design of sculptures which would fill even the narrow areas without a huge discrepancy in scale. As with most Greek sculpture, the original appearance was completely different from what we see today, because many details were added to the stone in paint. In fact, the backgrounds of the pediments, like the walls of ancient Babylon, were evidently painted bright blue. (Such facts were unnoted, or perhaps pointedly ignored, by the proponents of the stark white "classical style," which is a result, not of austere classical taste, but of centuries of weathering).

This oversize and colorful edifice was only the shell designed to hold the *piece de resistance*: the enormous sculpture of Zeus, made c. 430 BCE by the famous sculptor Pheidias who later created the statue of Athena Parthenos for the Acropolis of Athens. Zeus, seated on a throne and crowned with a wreath of olive, held a scepter topped with an eagle in his left hand, and a Winged Victory in his right. A statue of this type was known as chryselephantine (made of gold and ivory), although it was actually made of wood, and covered with ivory and gold sheets. The face was ivory, whereas the hair, the beard and the scepter were made of gold. The throne of Zeus and the base of the statue were decorated with painted mythical scenes, deities, and heroes in gold, ebony and precious stones.

This was the most famous statue of antiquity, immortalized as one of the Seven Wonders of the World.[14] Although we have a description of it by Pausanias and several coin representations, nothing of it has been preserved. After the end of the Olympic games (393 CE), it was transferred to Constantinople, where it was destroyed by fire in 475 CE. (Now if it had really been made of gold and ivory, it would not have burned so well. But then, perhaps the loot from Pisa could not finance that kind of expenditure).

The Temple of Olympian Zeus (Olympeion) in Athens

Classical temples are often massive, but even by the usual standard, this shrine of Zeus was enormous, the largest temple in Greece, exceeding even the Parthenon in size. Work began on it in 515 BCE during the reign of the tyrant Peisistratos, who was said to have initiated the building work to gain public favor, in which he evidently was somewhat lacking. Whether he achieved his aim is doubtful, as the temple was worked on sporadically until its completion in 132 CE by the Roman Emperor Hadrian.

The building was surrounded by 104 Pentelic marble Corinthian columns, each 17 meters (56 feet) high. 15 of the Corinthian columns remain standing to give a sense of the enormous size of the temple, which would have been approximately 96 x 40 meters (315 x 130 feet). The site also includes, as well as the remains of the Temple of Cronos and Rhea, ruins that are tentatively identified as the Temple of Apollo Delphinos, the Court of the Delphinion, and the Temple of Panhellenic Zeus.

Inspired by the long-awaited completion of the temple of Zeus, the Athenians honored Hadrian by building an arched gateway in the northwest corner of the sanctuary in 131 CE. The arch, also built of Pentelic marble, bears two inscriptions that bear mute witness to the Roman passion for exact footnotes. The one on the west facade facing the Acropolis reads "This is Athens, the ancient city of Theseus" while the other, on the side facing the sanctuary and the extension of the city by Hadrian, reads, "This is the city of Hadrian and not of Theseus".

1. B. Temples of Jupiter

Temple of Jupiter Stator

The Romans, practical in religion as in almost everything else, tended to build shrines to the gods as a reward for some answered petition.

Romulus, founder of Rome, promised to build a sanctuary to Jupiter Stator, "The Stayer," if the god made the fleeing Romans stand against the Sabines. Evidently Jupiter complied, as Romulus was triumphant and Jupiter got his edifice. This sanctuary was probably not an aedes, or a temple building; more likely, it was an altar enclosed by a low wall or fence.

In 294 BCE Marcus Atilius Regulus, who had made a similar vow in a similar situation, evidently with similar results, constructed an aedes or a temple building, on the site of the archaic altar. Scholars would dearly love to know exactly where the Temple of Jupiter Stator stood. Written sources say it was near or just outside the Porta Mugonia (we don't know where that was, either). When a medieval tower was demolished in 1827 beside the Arch of Titus on the north slope of the Palatine Hill, the ruins of an ancient building were found which have been identified by the hopeful as the foundations of the Temple of Jupiter Stator. Wherever it may have been, thanks to pictorial representations we have some idea what looked like; evidently it was similar to the Temple of the Olympian Zeus, featuring a giant chryselephantine statue. (In some representations, Jupiter's statue is depicted with a red face, but this is an attribute of his exalted state, not a reflection on his exploits).

The Temple of Capitoline Jupiter

This edifice, sensibly named for its location on the Capitoline Hill, was dedicated to Jupiter Optimus Maximus (Best and Greatest), together with Juno and Minerva, the other two divinities that made up the Capitoline Triad (three major deities). The twelve Dii Consentes were led by the

Capitoline Triad, whose rites from earliest times were conducted in the Capitoleum Vetus (Ancient Capitol) on the Capitoline Hill. (In the earliest period of the Roman Kingdom the Triad consisted of Jupiter, Mars and Quirinus, but later, probably as a result of Etruscan influence, the Triad became Jupiter, Juno Regina and Minerva). The Temple was begun by Tarquinius Priscus and completed by the last king of Rome, Tarquinius Superbus, both of whom were Etruscan 'foreign' kings. (The temple was only inaugurated, however, at the beginning of the Republican era in 509 BCE, when Tarquinius Superbus and his ilk had been booted out). Standing on a high podium with an entrance staircase at the front, it was probably surrounded by a colonnade on three sides, with two rows of pillars in line with those on the façade of the deep entrance porch outside the three long, narrow cells, dedicated to the three gods. The remains of enormous parallel walls show the sheer size of temple's base (about 55 x 60 m). On the roof was a splendid terracotta horse-drawn chariot commissioned by Tarquinius Superbus and made by the Etruscan artist Vulca of Veius in the sixth century BCE; at the beginning of the third century BCE during one of Rome's many facelifts the temple of tufa stone was rebuilt in marble and the roof got a new statue of bronze. The large square in front of the temple (the Area Capitolina) featured a number of temples dedicated to minor divinities, in addition to other religious buildings, statues and trophies. This was not only the most important sanctuary in Rome; it was also the center of political life. Here official offerings were made, treaties were signed and wars were declared, and here the triumphant generals of the Roman army came to give their thanks.

2. A. Temples of Hera

Heraeum at Argos

Argos, an ancient city that stood on the southern part of the peninsula of Greece, was a major seat of Hera worship. Pausanius explains that many suppliants sought the Heraeum, or holy place of Hera. It included a brook with the interesting name of Water of Freedom, useful for purification and secret sacrifices. The central feature of the place, however, was a huge statue made of gold and ivory by Polycleitus, of Hera, wearing a crown with Graces and Seasons worked upon it, and carrying in one hand a pomegranate connected with the holy mysteries and in the other a scepter topped by a cuckoo, symbol of Zeus' long-ago wooing. (Pausanias, *Description of Greece, II*) Nearby sat a much older and smaller image of Hera made of wild-pear wood that was brought from Tiryns when the Argives destroyed that city. (Deities of a conquered city were carried away as part of the loot and displayed as trophies. Obviously, they were not powerful or dangerous, as they had failed to defend their respective homelands, so they made nice souvenirs).

Temples of Hera at Samos

At Samos the worshippers of Hera expressed themselves in two Temples of Hera, sensibly called the First Temple of Hera at Samos, and the Second Temple of Hera at Samos. These very early specimens bore little resemblance to those marble mammoths built later. The first temple, built in the first half of the eighth century BCE, was a simple rectangular hall 100 feet long, with posts down the middle. Later, wooden posts with circular stone bases were added around the four sides. (This embryonic portico evidently evolved into the characteristic white columns of later Greek temples.) The walls of this early edifice were evidently made with whatever the faithful could find: there were two kinds of stones with little binding, and neither the roofs nor the columns were made of durable materials. The second temple, built at the same site in the middle of the seventh century BCE, was similar to the first, with two exceptions: there was no central row of columns, and the portico was built at the beginning. The roof was still made of clay, and the columns were still made of wood.

The Temple of Hera at Olympia

Before the construction of the temple of Zeus the only temple at Olympia was the modest Heraion dedicated to Hera, which was located in the northwest corner of the later sanctuary at Olympia and held statues of Hera, Zeus, and Hermes. This was another venture into sanctuary building that did not prove to be very durable, as its wooden columns rotted; the faithful replaced them with fieldstone and shell limestone. Sturdy it might not have been, but this temple of Hera had an interesting feature that is generally associated with the Parthenon built later for Athena: it was built in a system of regular and very exact proportions, so that the parts related to one another harmoniously. The width-to-length ratio of the temple was 3:8, and the number of pillars seen from the front and back (6) and the number seen from the sides (16) were in the same proportion. Also, the height of the columns was half the width of the temple's cella (internal chamber). Built about one hundred years before the Temple to Zeus, it was the oldest temple of its kind in all of Greece.

2. B. Temples of Juno

Temple of Juno Moneta

This temple was the result of one of those warrior vows, this one taken by L. Furius Camillus during the war against the Auruncii; it was built on the Arx (fortified part of the Capitoline Hill) in 344 BCE. Ancient sources, discussing that business about Juno's sacred geese that wakened the Romans during the Gallic siege of 390 BCE, appear to suggest the existence of a previous temple building. The remains of a square wall, which have been preserved in the same area and which some scholars have attributed to the fortification work of the Arx, might possibly go back to early phases of the Juno Moneta Temple. In addition, two archaic terracotta architectural artifacts found on the hill and dating to the end of the sixth or the beginning of the fifth century BCE could be from this temple. As has been said, this epithet may refer to the Juno's penchant for warning (as in the case of the sacred geese), but it was later to lend itself to the name of the nearby workshop responsible for minting coins which thenceforth also became known as Moneta.

Temple on the Esquiline

Juno Lucina was associated with light and childbirth. Her name Lucina recalls the Latin word lucis (light) but Livy records that the (lucus) grove on the Esquiline Hill, in which a temple was dedicated to her in 375 BCE, is the origin of her name. The primary feast of Juno Lucina, called the Matronalia, was celebrated on March 1. On this day, lambs and other beasts were sacrificed to her. The first of each month, the Kalends,[15] was sacred to Juno. The month of June, named for her, became very popular with brides. (Considering her own rocky matrimonial history, one wonders if this was altogether wise.)

Temple of Capitoline Jupiter

As has already been mentioned, Juno as well as Minerva had her share in the Temple of Capitoline Jupiter which was dedicated to the Capitoline Triad.

3. A. Temples of Poseidon

Temple of Poseidon at Sounion

Sounion is a small promontory at the tip of Attica overlooking the Aegean Sea. Sailors making their perilous way across this somewhat temperamental body of water have always found points of reference useful, and the lofty Temple of Poseison provides one today much as it did in antiquity. The temple, destroyed by the Persians in 480 BCE, was rebuilt later in the same century and continued to be one of the most important sanctuaries in Attica. "Sounion Hiron" (sanctuary of Sounion) was mentioned in the *Odyssey* as the place where Menelaus stopped during his return from Troy to bury his helmsman, Phrontes Onetorides. Architectural finds prove the existence of organized worship in the 7th and 6th centuries BCE on two points of the promontory: at the southern edge where the sanctuary of Poseidon was situated, and at the Sanctuary of Athena Sounias, located slightly to the northeast of the Sanctuary of Poseidon. Both sanctuaries remained simple until, at the beginning of the 5th century BCE, the Athenians included the Temple of Poseidon in their ambitious building projects. Their construction activities suffered a rude interruption because of the invading Persians in 480 BCE. Sounion, like the rest of Attica, flourished later, however, and important building was undertaken at both sanctuaries. From the 1st century BCE onwards, the sanctuaries gradually declined, and Pausanias, who sailed along the coast of the promontory in the mid-2nd century CE, confused the two temples and believed that the prominent temple on the top of the hill was that of Athena. That the site of the temple was known through the centuries is proved by descriptions of travelers as well as by graffiti on the stones, one example of which was contributed by Lord Byron (evidently the ancient gods were no longer dealing with hubris as it deserved, or Byron might have become an interesting exhibit of fauna or even flora).

3. B. Temples of Neptune
Temple near Flaminian Circus

The Neptune myth always involved the creation of the horse, and in early Rome he was held in high regard as Neptune Equestor, the god and patron of horses. Once horse races were established, his popularity was assured. He had an altar near the Flaminian Circus, the large race-track near which the equites, members of the equestrian class, mustered for their ceremonies, since only patricians (aristocrats) might hold ceremonies inside the pomerium, or ceremonial boundary of the city. Livy, in relating the prodigies of 206 BCE (*XXVIII.1.4*) described this statue as sweating. Cassius Dio (*LVII.60*), implying that this altar stood in a temple, mentions the same phenomenon. (Perhaps such was to be expected of a god who not only represented two kinds of natural waters but who also had charge of horse races). Neptune had a habit of manifesting himself in flooding spring rains in areas around the Circus Flaminius and the Pantheon. (Perhaps his sweating statue was a result of high humidity rather than an excess of activity). A coin issued around 40 BCE depicted the Neptune temple at the Circus Flaminius on a podium without an approaching staircase, and this has led to conjecture that the temple might only have been used during floods when it would be approached by boats. (Smith's *Dictionary of Greek & Roman Antiquities*)

A coin of Cn. Domitius Ahenobarbus, struck between 42 and 38 BCE, shows a temple with the legend Nept. Cn. Domitius M. f. Imp.('**Neptuno Gnaeus Domitius Marci filius Imperator**' --to Neptune Cnaeus Domitius son of Marcus and victorious general [dedicates]). This indicates that the temple was vowed at least between 42 and 38, but it may not have been built before 32, when Domitius had overcome some tiff with Augustus and was holding the consulship. It is impossible to determine whether Domitius built an entirely new temple, or restored that which previously existed in the Circus Flaminius.

Temple in Campus Martius

Marcus Vipsanius Agrippa, Augustus's military Chief of Staff and his Admiral, won a naval victory over Marc Antony at the decisive battle of Actium in 31 BCE, which firmly established Augustus' power. Agrippa went on a major architectural spree, building his famous Pantheon and baths. Between them he dedicated a temple and porticus to Neptune. After it was dedicated in 25 BCE, the porticus may have been the center for the public aspects of the Neptunalia. (Agrippa not only built the temples, but coins honoring Agrippa routinely featured Neptune; after all, his defeat of Marc Antony at sea, which assured that his dear friend Octavian would become Augustus, was a development worthy of a great deal of maritime gratitude.) This Neptune complex was completely restructured by Hadrian when he also rebuilt the Pantheon, so it is difficult to discern the Agrippan design and functions of the structure. (Platner, Topographical Dictionary of Ancient Rome, *"Ara et Aedes Neptuni", pp 360-361*).

Neptune's festival, celebrated on July 23, and sensibly called the Neptunalia, honored him as the god of water in general. At this time of year when rivers were low and water was most scarce, Romans sought Neptune's protection of irrigation waters and works. Neptunalia was also considered to be an auspicious day to start new irrigation works, which, despite the heat, were easier to construct in summer than during wetter seasons. To honor the god, the Romans went out to the fields and forests and built small huts called **umbrae** (shades) or **tabernaculi** (tabernacles) out of leafy laurel (or bay) branches (in July in Italy, who can blame them?). Within the shade of these natural tents they feasted, sacrificing a bull to the god and sharing the meat with him, drinking spring water as well as wine to keep cool in these hot summer days. It was hoped that such piety would assure rainfall for the crops and forestall any drought. The Neptunalia was originally mostly a private affair concerned with Neptune's protection of fresh agricultural water, but when Agrippa dedicated his temple and porticus to Neptune celebrating that aforesaid naval victory over Marc Antony, it developed into a public observance.

4. A. Temples of Pluto

No one was especially eager to build great temples to Pluto, the most dreadful of the gods, as people were a bit leery of attracting his attention. At Eleusis among the great sanctuaries of Demeter and Persephone (about which more later) all he got was in the way of a Plutonium was a small temple and, built into the base of the rocky hill overlooking the temple complex, a grotto whose subterranean opening is still visible today. This "Pluto Hole" was supposed to be the opening through which he abducted Persephone. (We have seen that various poets had their own ideas about where this celebrated crime took place). Although Asia Minor was filled with magnificent temples to the gods, in the centre of the city of Hierapolis Pluto once again received only a small subterranean cavern, situated this time next to the great temple of Apollo. This Plutonium or Gate of Hades or "Devil's Hole" was commonly regarded as a passageway to the underworld. Poisonous gases emanated from the hole and instantly killed any animals that wandered in. The priests of Apollo, who apparently held their breath or had some other means of breathing fresh air, impressed people mightily by going into the hole and coming out again unharmed, as this gave them the appearance of having power over death.

4. B. Temple of Roman Pluto

About the best Rome had to offer the Dark Lord (besides a share in the Pantheon, dedicated to all the gods) was a small rectangular building called the Temple of Pluto in Hadrian's huge villa complex outside Rome. Since all that remains of this edifice are mosaic fragments and some walls, it doesn't tell us a great deal. Old maps show a rectangular building with a central apse on one of its long sides. (Why Hadrian, the most peaceful of Roman Emperors, wanted to honor Death Personified remains a mystery).

5. A. Temples of Hestia

As Hestia was basically the guardian of Prometheus's priceless gift of fire, she wound up on the short end of the temple building for a different reason. Her special sanctuary was in the *prytaneum*.or *prytaneion*, the public hall regarded as the city center, which featured a perpetually burning civic hearth-fire. This fire was the civic core, just as the hearth was the core of a home. (In these days before matches and lighter fluid, starting a fire was a major concern. When a city-state sent out a colony, the emigrants took great care to get a new civic fire started from a coal brought from the parent city). Around this cheery divine symbol political life and ceremonies took place, and foreign dignitaries and outstanding citizens were entertained. The actual shrine of Hestia was in an inner chamber where an eternal sacred flame, symbolizing the very life of the community, burned. The Curetes, the priestesses of Hestia, were in charge of this sacred conflagration, which periodically was rekindled from altars that Greeks considered most pure, those of Apollo at Delphi or Delos. (Carrying a live fire from Delphi or Delos to outlying Greek cities must have been a severe test of devotees' ingenuity and fortitude).

The *prytaneum* was Hestia's home, but a few special temples were dedicated to her. In Ephesus, the Temple of Hestia Boulaia was annexed to the *Prytaneion* and the sacred fire was attended by priests called Pritanei. Athens, which generally had a large population of sculptors, had a statue of Hestia in its *prytaneion*, but, as most cities contented themselves with representing her by the flame. (She certainly would have been scandalized if portrayed hunting like Artemis or going around half-clothed like Aphrodite). The Giustiniani Vesta in the Torlonia Museum shows Hestia or Vesta standing upright, simply robed, a hood over her head, the left hand raised and pointing upwards.

5. B Temples of Vesta

In the Roman Forum was the round Aedes Vestae, attributed to King Numa Pompilius, who transferred the worship of Vesta to Rome (Livy *I. 20*, and Ovid, *Fasti, III. 46*) from Alba Longa, the oldest of the Latin colonies in Latium. Numa, being a sensible man, also transferred the four Vestal Virgins, the chaste priestesses who took care of Vesta's home and, most importantly, her fire. (Plutarch *Numa, 10*). One of the later kings increased the number of Vestals to six (Plutarch *Numa, 10*). In the small but rich **Aedes Vestae** (the shrine of Vesta was not a *templum*, in the strict

Roman sense; since it was holy in the first place from the presence of Vesta's flame, it was never consecrated by the augurs, being above such necessities) the sacred fire of the Roman state burned until 394 CE, maintained by the Vestal Virgins and renewed at the start of the new Roman year, March 1. Nearby was the lovely **Atrium Vestae**, the Home of the Vestals, a large and exceptionally magnificent edifice.

Aedes Vestae

The Vestals possessed not only fine buildings but great honor. They were given the place of honor at public games and festivals, but they had power as well as prestige. On their way through the streets of Rome, they were preceded by the lictors, bearers of the **fasces**. As this was a bundle of rods (twigs) tied together, out of which an axe projected, it may not sound very impressive, but it was a symbol of sovereign power, and only Rome's highest magistrates shared this honor with the Vestals.(This particular honor must have made getting through Rome's crowded streets easier, which was a major boon in itself).

Vestals alone among women could make a will, as they controlled their property; they also kept wills and important papers for great men. If a Vestal met a criminal on the way to execution, she could order him to be set free. As one may imagine from the above, insulting a Vestal was a capital crime (which only a fool would indulge in anyway, considering the benefits they could offer).

During the Republic there were six Vestals. Two between the ages of six and sixteen were in training. Two between sixteen and twenty-six carried out the sacred duties of keeping the holy fire on the altar of Vesta burning, bringing fresh water daily from the fountain Egeria, and serving as custodian of the sacred Palladium, a small wooden statue of Minerva, supposedly brought from Troy. The two "Senior Vestals," between twenty-six and thirty-six, taught the young ones. One of these last was named the Virgo Vestalis Maxima, and, having power over the powerful, she was definitely a force to be reckoned with. Vestals of good character could marry after their thirty years of service (Vestals of bad character, if found out, had already been buried alive in the Campus Sceleris [Field of the Wicked]). When there was an opening in the college of Vestals due to the death or retirement of one Vestal, another between six and ten years of age would be chosen by lot from Roman families in good standing. The chief priest, or Pontifex Maximus,[16] (who lived and officiated in his official sanctuary, the Regia, adjacent to the Vestals' house) would then go to the girl's home, take her by the hand, and repeat a ritual sentence, "I take you, Amata, as a Vestal." The girls were always called Amata at their choosing, supposedly because this had been the name of the first Vestal. The new "Amata," who now lived in the house of the Vestals, was no longer subject to her father, but instead was subject to the college of priests. (Hardly a change for the better, if the girl had an unruly streak. But, as we have seen, Vestals with unruly streaks did not prosper).

The festival Vestalia was observed from June 7 - 15. On the first day of this festival, the **penus Vestae** or the inner sanctum of the Vesta temple which was kept closed the entire year, was opened for women who came to bring offerings bare-footed. The temple was ritually cleansed on the last day.

6. A. Temples of Athena

Athena had many grand temples; we shall take a quick look at the most famous of them all on the Acropolis (High Place of the City) of Athens, and then at her well-traveled small images. Never a city to do things shabbily, Athens on its Acropolis had two large temples dedicated to Athena, dating from the 6th century BCE, in positions that had probably contained older shrines before them. The rampaging Persians (evidently in the same exuberant invasion that had such a bad effect down at Sounion) destroyed these temples in 480 BCE, and some forty years later the Athenian leader Pericles commissioned the sculptor Pheidias to construct a new and magnificent temple for Athena Parthenos (Maiden). Pheidias, carrying out the commission with enthusiasm, created the Parthenon, crowning glory of Athens and universal symbol of Greek civilization. Built by the architects Ictinus and Callicrates under Pheidias' supervision, the temple is generally considered to be the finest example of the Doric order, the simplest of the three classical Greek architectural styles. Pheidias was a devotee of the golden ratio of 1 to .618, (sometimes approximated as 8 to 5) for length to width ratio of rectangles. (This ratio, which seems the most pleasing to the human eye, is ubiquitous in nature and man-made objects such as the Temple of Hera mentioned earlier, and Pheidias [or Phidias] used it so much that its central numeric value "phi" is said to be named for him.) In the Parthenon, where this principle is everywhere applied, the exterior dimensions form a perfect golden rectangle and there are golden rectangles throughout the temple; even the spaces between the columns form golden rectangles. Also, the front elevation is roughly 1.618 times as wide as it is tall. No effort was spared on the Parthenon's decoration as well: sculpture inside and outside the building was the finest Greece could produce, and as a finishing touch the building was brightly painted. (As was mentioned earlier, centuries of weathering, with the help of the depredations of various visitors, has removed the paint, leaving us with that "classical white" which moderns admire and which would look just plain unfinished to the Greeks). The whole was topped off with colorful terra cotta roof tiles.

(The central cella of the temple sheltered Pheidias' forty foot high standing chryselephantine statue of Athena, holding the small statue of

Nike [victory] she held in her right hand. This last feature is probably a sculptural boast concerning the victories over those temple-flattening Persians). After a varied life including reincarnations as Christian church and mosque, the Parthenon was looking good until 1687, when the Turks used it as a powder magazine in their nasty little war with Venice. A Venetian bomb fell on the temple, and the result was not happy. What was left was looted at the beginning of the 19th century the British ambassador to Constantinople, Lord Elgin, who carried most of the sculptural decorations of the monument off to England and sold them to the British Museum, where (much to the dismay of modern Greeks) they are still exhibited.

The Palladium was a sacred image kept in the temple of Athena at Troy, supposedly a likeness of her. According to legend, the image was sent by Zeus to Dardanus, the founder of Troy, and the city could not be taken while it possessed the Palladium. During the Trojan War it disappeared. Some say two Greeks, Diomed and Odysseus, stole it. Others say that during the sack of Troy, Ajax the Lesser carried it off. The Romans, who later claimed to have the true Palladium in their temple of the Vestal Virgins, said that Aeneas took it when he fled Troy. But many cities, including Argos, Athens, and Luceria, owned such images, all of which came to be known as Palladia.

6. B. Temples of Minerva

Minerva had many temples, in Rome and scattered throughout the entire Roman world, but most of them, being in even worse shape than those of Athena, are hard to identify. Oldest of course was the sanctuary shared with Jupiter and Juno on the Capitoline Hill of Rome. (Jupiter naturally had the cella in the center, Minerva got the one on the right, and Juno had to be content with the one on the left). Minerva had also a temple on the Aventine Hill. This was a meeting-place for dramatic poets and actors, who were organized into guilds under her patronage. Her special holiday the Quinquatrus, so called because it fell on the fifth day after the Ides, [14] was held from March 19 to 23, coinciding with the spring equinox. All the schools had holidays at this time (Spring Break thus has excellent historical precedent), and the pupils on reassembling brought a fee (minerval) to the teachers (a custom which unhappily, at least from the teacher's viewpoint, has disappeared). Every house celebrated this holiday, for Minerva was patron of the women's weaving and spinning and the workmen's crafts.

According to Ovid, there were gladiatorial shows during the last four days of the festival because Minerva was the goddess of war (Ovid, *Fasti, III. 809-834*; Juvenal *X. 115*). Some sources say, however, that she shared this holiday with the war god Mars (which arrangement was unlikely to make either deity happy, as they were said to detest each other).

Around 50 BCE Pompey the Great built a temple to Minerva Victrix (conqueror) out of the spoils of his eastern conquests. (Today the ruins of this temple are underneath a Gothic Christian Church, which is very accurately named the Santa Maria sopra Minerva.) In Minerva's temple on the Caelian Hill, where for reasons no one has ever explained she was worshipped as Minerva Capta, the captive, a festival called the lesser Quinquatrus was celebrated on the 13th and 14th of June, chiefly by the flute-players, as she was said to have invented the flute (which as we have said she didn't keep, but flute-players honored her anyway). (Livy *IX. 30*; Ovid, *Fasti, VI. 651*).

7. A. Temples of Apollo

Temple of Apollo at Delphi

Although Apollo had magnificent temples all through the Mediterranean world, this was his chief oracular shrine, which he was said to have seized, while still an infant, by killing its guardian, the serpent Python, a violent event that was celebrated every eight years in the festival of the Stepteria. Apollo's priestess, called the Pythia, became the most famous and respected oracle in the ancient world. As she always prophesied in a state of frenzy, priests of Apollo were standing nearby ready to interpret her ravings as the enigmatic prophecies of the god. (These far-from-specific interpretations were often capable of being interpreted in two exactly opposite ways, a fact which may have been of minimal help to worshippers, but which helped maintain the oracle's reputation for infallibility.)

The ancient hymns name Apollo as the architect of his own temple. "The lord Phoebus Apollo came to Crisa beneath white Parnassus, where a cliff overhangs from above and a hollow, rugged glade runs under. There he said, "In this place I intend to build a glorious temple to be an oracle for men who dwell in Peloponnesus, as well as the men from Europe and from all the sea-touched isles who will come to question me. In my temple I will give them infallible counsel." Then Phoebus Apollo laid out all the foundations throughout, wide and very long; and upon these the sons of Erginus, Trophonius and Agamedes, dear to the immortals, laid a footing of stone. And the countless tribes of men built the whole temple of wrought stones, to be sung of for ever." (*Homeric Hymn to Apollo, 280-299*) (We note that Apollo contented himself with the general laying out of the plan. The dirty work was left to the mortals).

Said mortals did their work very well. Built in a breathtaking natural site halfway up Mount Parnassus, the main **temenos** (sacred space) contained numerous monuments. The Sacred Way led through the precinct to the altar and temple of Apollo. Other buildings included a theater, a stadium, and numerous treasuries erected to house the rich gifts brought by the many truth-seekers. Delphi came to be regarded as the center of the world, and the fame of its oracle extended beyond the borders of Greece and gave it international standing, in contrast to the sanctuary of Olympia, which had a more national Greek character. The festival of the Pythian Games, one of the four great athletic and drama festivals of ancient Greece, was held every four years in this picturesque location.

7. B. Temples of Roman Apollo

Temple of Apollo Medicus

Apollo had two famous temples in Rome. The first, to Apollo Medicus, vowed in 433 BCE because of a raging plague in the city (Livy *IV.25.3*), was built in the Campus Martius and dedicated in 431 by the consul Cn. Julius (Livy *IV.29.7*). Nearby was an earlier cult centre of the god, the Apollinar, which was either a grove or an altar. When Caius Sosius, governor of Cilicia and Syria, rebuilt the sanctuary in 34 BCE in marble, it became known as the Temple of Apollo Sosianus. According to Pliny the Elder (*Natural History XXXV and XXXVI*) this temple was a museum of artistic treasures: an Apollo with lyre by Timarchides, a statue of Apollo of cedar wood, and the beautiful sculptured group of the Niobids (those unfortunate offspring of Queen Niobe), which even the ancients were doubtful whether they should ascribe to Scopas or Praxiteles. Cassius Dio (*Fragment 84.2*) informs us that at the death of the Younger Scipio the statue of Apollo (he does not say which one) shed tears for three days (which is a much more godly exhibition than Neptune's sweating). Standing today are three fluted columns with Corinthian capitals that belonged to the porch of the temple.

Temple of Apollo on the Palatine

Octavian Caesar, working his way toward becoming the Emperor Augustus, was always mindful of traditional Roman leaders, who had tended to build temples to the gods after some great victory. Offering up the good old Roman prayer of **do ut des** (I give so that you may give), in 36 BCE during his campaign against Sextus Pompeius Octavian vowed to build a temple to Apollo in Rome if he were successful. Having won his victory, on October 9, 28 BCE, according to Cassius Dio (*XLIX.15.5*), he fulfilled his promise and dedicated his **Aedes Apollinis** on the Palatine Hill on ground that had been struck by lightning and therefore had been made public property. (Exactly where on the Palatine Hill this edifice stood is a question happily debated by scholars for centuries). This, the most magnificent of Augustus' buildings, made a good start on the boast the aging Emperor would make that he found Rome a city of brick and left it a city of marble. Constructed of solid blocks of white Luna marble (Vergil, *Aeneid* vi.69; viii.720, and Ovid *Tristia* iii.1.60), it featured a chariot of the sun on the roof, many fine statues, and doors that were decorated with ivory reliefs, one representing the rescue of Delphi from the Celts, and the other the fate of those long-suffering Niobids (Propertius, *Elegiae, II, 31*). (The Romans always emphasized the story of Niobe in Apollo's temples, perhaps as a warning to beware the wrath of the Archer God). Before the entrance to the temple stood a marble statue of the god, and an altar surrounded by four oxen. In the cella was a statue of Apollo by Scopas, one of Diana by Timotheus, and of Leto by Cephisodotus. Pliny the Elder says that Augustus deposited golden gifts in the temple and his son in law Marcellus dedicated a collection of seal rings and jewels, hanging lamps, and a statue of Apollo Comaeus, brought to Rome in the time of Verus.

Also according to Propertius, the temple was connected with, and perhaps surrounded by, a porticus with columns of **giallo antico**, between which were statues of the fifty daughters of Danaus, and facing them equestrian statues of the ill-fated husbands they murdered on their wedding night, the sons of Aegyptus (it is perhaps unfortunate that these young men did not keep a close eye on their brides earlier). Adjoining, or perhaps forming a part of the **porticus**, was a library, **Bibliotheca Apollinis**, large enough for meetings of the senate (Cassius Dio *LIII 1.3*). It consisted of two sections, one for Greek and one for Latin books, with medallion portraits of famous writers on the walls. The space enclosed within the **porticus** was the **area aedis Apollinis.** The Sibylline books (what was left of them -- more about those tomes of literature later) were brought here from the temple of Jupiter on the Capitol and placed beneath the pedestal of the statue of Apollo (Vergil, *Aeneid VI. 72*. Part of the ceremony of the **ludi saeculares** took place at this temple until it was burned down on March 18, 363 CE.

As has been stated, the Cumaean Sibyl was not only the greatest of Apollo's Italian minions but apparently the laziest. If no one came to her cave to collect her prophecies, they were scattered by winds and never read. Evidently, at some point some of these complex enigmatic verses, called "Sibylline Leaves," were bound into books. The Sibyl herself in a burst of energy brought to Rome nine volumes of these prophecies, which she said contained the future of the world, offering them to King Tarquin **Superbus** (the Arrogant; he lived up to his name with enthusiasm) at an outrageous price. He scoffed, and she immediately burned three volumes, offering the remaining six at the same high price. Again he refused. She burned three volumes, and once more asked the original price. By this time Tarquin was wondering if he had been a bit hasty, and he purchased the remaining Sibylline books, which were carefully kept in the Capitoline Temple and consulted by the Senate when catastrophe threatened. Some were destroyed by fire in 83 BCE while the rest (or, according to some scholars, copies collected from similar oracles) survived until 405 CE, when they perished in one of those ubiquitous fires. After this second fire, Romans searched the world for replacements for the Sibylline Leaves. The Sibyl herself, it was discovered, had vanished (even Sibyls get to retire sometime). So the way was left clear for the production of pseudo-Sibylline prophecies, which enterprising souls kept supplying until the end of the Roman Empire.

7. C. Temples of Mithras

The temples of Mithras, or Mithraea, were found in adapted natural caves or in buildings imitating caves. They were dark and had no windows even if they were not actually underground, and were sometimes built under existing buildings. The entrance antechamber, called the *spelunca* (cave), had raised benches along the walls and a sanctuary, sometimes almost a separate alcove, at the far end, where the altar and the tauroctony, or pictoral representation of Mithras killing the bull, were always located. The pictures typically include a serpent, a dog, and a raven assisting Mithras and the torchbearers Cautes and Cautopates standing on either side. Above Mithras, the symbols for the sun and the moon are featured in a star-strewn night sky. Some scholars hold that the tauroctony is astrological, with Taurus the bull, Canis Major the dog and the other depictions representing Zodiac signs and the two torchbearers representing the equinoxes. A pictorial representation found at Housesteads in England, showing Mithras with the Twelve Signs of the Zodiac around him in an egg-shaped frame, supports this idea.

8. A. Temples of Artemis
The Haven of Artemis at Vravrona (Brauron)

A few miles outside Athens lies the temple complex of Vravrona, sometimes called "The Parthenon of the Bear Maidens," a site sacred to the huntress-goddess Artemis surrounding a long-revered holy spring. The temple contained many images of the children who once studied at the temple - Artemis' "little bears" or **arktoi** who danced for their goddess in sacred processions after the death of one of her special bears. Artemis' festival, the Brauronia, was held here. The tyrant Peisistratos, hailing from Brauron, made the worship of Artemis an official faith of Athens during his ascendency (although he carefully honored Athena with fine tributes).

The Brauron temple was finally abandoned after nature herself reclaimed it: the local river Erasimos flooded the grounds, and the surrounding area is still moist, if not actually swampy.

Iphigeneia, the ill-fated and well-traveled daughter of Agamemnon, is said to have come to it as a priestess of Artemis, bringing with her a wooden statue of the goddess that was enshrined here for many years. Local legend insists that she was "sacrificed" to a life in the temple and lived here until she died rather than being physically sacrificed so that the Greek ships could sail to Troy. A roofless cave is said to be the remains of her tomb.[17]

Though temples and clergy of Artemis were entirely female, served by women vowed to chastity, boy children were allowed to study at this temple, and their statues stand in the museum along with their female classmates. Possibly boy-girl twins were permitted in acknowledgement of the relationship between Artemis and her own twin brother, Apollo, or Iphigenia [15] and her brother, Orestes, who are credited in some tales with founding the site. At the festival of Artemis Orthiawhen, held at Sparta, young Spartan boys would try to steal cheeses from the altar, being whipped as they tried. The meaning of Orthia and the nature of the ritual whipping has been lost. Artemis was a goddess of the edges and boundaries in general: between virginity and marriage, culture and civilization, war and peace, birth and death. Among the epithets given to her are: Potnia Theron (mistress of wild animals), Kourotrophos (nurse of youths), Locheia (helper in childbirth), Agrotera (huntress), and Cynthia (taken from her birthplace on Mount Cynthus on Delos). One of her strongest identifications is with the boundary between youth and maturity; young girls reached puberty they were initiated into her cult, but when they decided to marry, they were asked to lay in front of her altar all the paraphernalia of their virginity, as well as toys, dolls and locks of their hair, as they were leaving the realm of the virgin goddess.

Temple of Artemis at Ephesus

"I have seen the walls and Hanging Gardens of ancient Babylon, the statue of Olympian Zeus, the Colossus of Rhodes, the high Pyramids and the tomb of Mausolus. But when I saw the temple at Ephesus rising to the clouds, all the other wonders were put in the shade." Philon of Byzantium, De Septem Orbis Spectaculis.

In Asia Minor, the unpretentious and chaste goddess of the woods underwent a startling transfiguration and became one of those Earth-Mother figures usually associated with Gaia, Rhea or even Aphrodite. She was honored in the ancient city of Ephesus in Asia Minor (Turkey) with a great marble temple that became one of the Seven Wonders of the World. Although the foundation of the temple dates back to the seventh century BCE, when a shrine was built to hold a sacred stone, (perhaps a meteorite), that had "fallen from Zeus," the structure that earned a spot in the Wonders List was first built around 550 BCE by Croesus, the extremely wealthy Lydian king. This temple, designed by Theodorus and featuring bronze statues sculpted by the most skilled artists of their time, Pheidias, Polycleitus, Kresilas, and Phradmon, was 300 feet in length and 150 feet wide with a magnificent courtyard before it. More than one hundred stone columns supported a massive roof. The new temple was the pride of Ephesus until 356 BCE when a young egomaniac by the name of Herostratus burned it so that he might be remembered. The Ephesians, understandably annoyed by this selfish attitude, declared the death penalty for anyone speaking the young egotist's name and set about rebuilding the temple.

The restored building is thought to be the first completely constructed of marble; its 36 columns whose lower portions were carved with figures in high-relief were outstanding, and it housed many works of art, but much of its splendor came from its sheer size. Pliny the Elder recorded its length as 425 feet and the width as 225 feet. Some 127 columns, 60 feet in height, supported the roof. In comparison, the Parthenon was a mere 230 feet long, 100 feet wide and had only 58 columns.

According to Pliny, construction took 120 years, though some experts suspect he exaggerated, and that the structure was actually hastily erected in a mere 50 or 60 years. When Alexander the Great, always on the lookout for a little glory, came to Ephesus in 333 BCE and saw the temple under construction, he offered to finance the completion if the city would credit him as the builder. The city fathers didn't want Alexander's name carved on the temple, but they were well aware that refusing this young conqueror could be deadly. Their answer was worthy of the Delphic oracle, "It is not fitting that one god should build a temple for another god." Alexander's ego was flattered, the temple was completed without advertising, and Ephesus remained standing as Alexander marched away to pick on somebody else.

Pliny reported that earthen ramps were employed to get the heavy stone beams perched on top of the columns. This method had a little hiccup when one of the largest beams, put into position above the door, went down crookedly and the architect could find no way to get it to lie flat. Sick with worry, he finally fell asleep and the Goddess appeared to him saying that she herself had moved the stone in the proper position. The next morning the architect found that the beam had settled into its proper place during the night. (Architects throughout the centuries, who have received no such aid, could be pardoned for a bit of jealousy).

For several hundred years, the sanctuary served as both a marketplace and a religious institution, being visited by merchants, tourists, artisans, and kings who paid homage to the goddess by sharing their profits with her. Recent archeological excavations at the site revealed gifts from pilgrims including statuettes of Artemis made of gold and ivory as well as earrings, bracelets, and necklaces... artifacts from as far away as Persia and India. There was also a booming souvenir business in miniature Artemis idols, as Paul the Christian missionary learned when in 57 CE he won so many converts to his new religion that the silversmiths' union, fearing an economic downturn, threatened to deprive Christianity of its foremost missionary. (Cooler heads prevailed, for once, and Paul escaped).

8. B. Temples of Diana

The Roman goddess Diana, usually portrayed as a huntress accompanied by a deer, had as her greatest sanctuary the grove of Diana Nemorensis ("Diana of the Wood") on the shores of Lake Nemi at Aricia, near Rome, a shrine common to the cities of the Latin League. Associated with Diana at Aricia were the hero Virbius, who was said to have been the first priest of

Diana's cult at Aricia, and Egeria, the spirit of a nearby spring who shared with Diana the guardianship of childbirth. (Egeria, according to Livy [*I, 21*], was the wife of the second king of Rome, Numa Pompilius, who claimed to consult her secretly at night and then loftily informed the Romans of the religious precepts and observances which they would hereafter follow at the behest of his divine wife and her advisers, the Camenae or Muses. In a burst of cynicism the historian says that this was a political ploy on the part of the king to put the fear of Heaven [or some other supernatural region] into recalcitrant Romans [Livy *I, 19*].) While Egeria was the helpful, if somewhat soggy, wife of an early Roman king, Virbius was even more unusual. Ancient custom dictated that the priest of Diana at Aricia must be a runaway slave and that he must slay his predecessor in combat. This leads piquant speculation about Virbius' origin and the demise by which he evidently achieved an immortal state.

Strangely enough this unique and violent shrine was not only a place of worship, but of healing as well, because of waters which came from a spring (evidently not that of Egeria, which was nearer Rome) originating in the lava rocks at Nemi, and falling in cascades into the lake at a place called "Le Mole." Here Diana was worshipped as Diana Lucina (of the light) and torch-bearing processions were held in her honor in Nemi wood.

At Rome the most important temple of Diana, said to date back to the 6th century BCE, was on the Aventine Hill. Though Jupiter had some duties related to the Latin League, Diana was the goddess of the Latin commonwealth, and her temple housed the foundation charter of the Latin League. Diana was also considered the protector of the lower classes and slaves; slaves could also ask for asylum in her temple, and the Ides (13th) of August, her festival at Rome and Aricia, was a holiday for slaves.

9. A. Temples of Aphrodite

The great centers of Aphrodite worship remained on the islands of Cyprus and Cythera, from which she seems to have come to mainland Greece, and in Asia Minor. The city of Aphrodisias in Asia Minor was dedicated to her, and she had great temples on the islands mentioned above as well as islands such as Rhodes. (One can well imagine what scandalous doings went on in such temples).

In mainland Greece, however, she had sanctuaries in most cities, and in Corinth a magnificent one at the highest point of the acropolis, called the Acrocorinth. She also had temples in Athens, several with very fine statues, and others near the sea, as she was protectress of sailors. In Sparta Pausanias (*3, 12-18*) mentions several places and one two-story temple dedicated to Aphrodite. It is perhaps not surprising that the wooden images of Aphrodite in this belligerent city carried war arms.

9. B. Temples of Venus

As mentioned before, Venus Cloacina (Venus of the Sewer) was venerated from very early Roman times. The very ancient and remarkable shrine to Venus Cloacina, sometimes ascribed to the mythical Italian leader Titus Tatius, [16] is generally thought to have been built in gratitude for the Cloaca Maxima, the first sewer in Rome and possibly the first in the Western World (Titius Tatius and the Cloaca Maxima don't belong to the same era, but legend never worries about such details). To understand the Romans' thankfulness one has only to imagine a hot day in a large city which had no sewer (the Cloaca Maxima seems in the beginning to have been an open ditch -- not a pretty thought, but, as it drained the Forum area and made the Forum possible, it was very useful).

A temple to Venus dating back to 293 BCE was inaugurated on August 18, and as a result, on this date the Vinalia Rustica was observed. The Veneralia festival was celebrated on April 1 in honor of Venus Verticordia, guardian of chastity (as has been mentioned, this is an interesting duty, considering how little her activities usually had to do with this attribute). After the Roman defeat near Lake Trasimenus in 215 BCE, a temple was built on the Capitoline for Venus Erycina. This temple was officially opened on April 23, and a festival, the Vinalia Priora, was instituted to celebrate the occasion.

One of the more unusual shrines to Venus was built by Pompey the Great. In 55 BCE when he was building the first permanent theater in Rome, he encountered great criticism for spending so much money and marble on a place of entertainment, so he built a small "temple to Venus" into the edifice. (Venus seems to have accepted being used in this way; after all, theater productions often depict some of her favorite ideas).

Julius Caesar, who claimed that his Julian line descended from Iulus, the son of Aeneas, built a white marble temple to his supposed progenitress in the center of his Julian Forum and had much to do with the expansion of her cult (both formally and informally).

The gigantic Temple of Venus and Rome at the edge of the Roman Forum was designed by Emperor Hadrian and dedicated to the patron goddesses of Rome: Roma, the divine personification of the city, and Venus, the mother of Aeneas, ancestor of Romulus and Remus.

10. A. Temple of Ares

Ares was an ancestral deity of Thebes, but Greater Greece was usually wary of him. He had long been identified with the Areopagus, or 'Hill of Ares' in Athens, where as we have seen he was alleged to have stood trial. The Temple of Ares in the Agora of Athens has been dated from ceramic evidence in its foundations to the end of the first century BCE. This was not a new construction, but a fifth-century Doric peripteral temple, possibly from Acharnae, that was taken apart piece by piece and moved to the Agora.

10. B. Temple of Mars

Mars, father of Romulus and god of war, had a huge temple in Rome called the 'Mars Gradivus'("he who precedes the army in battle"), where Roman army gathered before leaving for battle. Another great edifice of his was the temple of Mars Ultor ("the avenger"), located in the Forum Augustus. The Campus Martius ("field of Mars"), situated beyond the city walls, was also dedicated to him. Here the army was drilled and athletes were trained. In the Regia on the Forum Romanum, the 'hastae Martiae' ("lances of Mars") were kept. When these lances 'moved', it was seen as a portent of war. The commander who was to lead the army into battle moved the lances while saying 'Mars, vigila!' ("Mars awaken"), as the deity was evidently prone to naps. As Mars Gradivus, the aroused god was supposed to go forth before the army and led them to victory. (Considering Rome's long and largely successful history, he seems to have done an excellent job of this).

The Romans named the first month of their year March (Martius) after Mars, and celebrated him on March 1st, the 'Feriae Marti' and October 19th, the 'Armilustrium,' when all weapons were ritually cleaned and put away for the coming winter. In addition, there were the Equirria on February 27 and March 14, on which horse races were held. The Quinquatrus, which as has been said, he shared with Minerva, was the five-day celebration during the vernal equinox, at the end of which was the Tubilustrium on March 23, on which weapons and war-trumpets were cleansed. Mars' special priest was called the **flamen Martialis**, but there were also priests of Mars, whom he shared with his troublesome archaic counterpart Quirinus, called the **Salii** ("jumpers"), because of the procession through the streets of the city in which they jumped the entire way singing the **Carmen Saliare**. (There are many indications that ancient priests must have been athletic and sometimes frenetic).

11. A. Temple of Hermes

Hermes had few temples, as the Greeks generally preferred to represent him by statues, sometimes in a gymnasium. This is logical, as *Orphic Hymn 28 to Hermes* calls him "great life-supporter, who rejoices in arts gymnastic, (it goes on to add, less comfortingly, "and in fraud divine.") His statue was also placed on the open street, and in Athens, outside houses for good luck. Often these **"Hermai"** were not even statues in the usual sense. Pausanias tells us (*10.12.6*) that in Khrysa in Troas there is a Hermes beside the grave of the Sibylla Herophile which is "a square shaped figure of stone." (Of course, for a god who began in the pre-Hellenic days with a name that means a square or rectangular pillar of stone, or even "a pile of marker stones," perhaps that isn't too bad).

Pausanias also says, "At the Arcadian gate of Ithome, Messenia, leading to Megalopolis is a Herma of Attic style; for the square form of Herma is Athenian, and the rest adopted it thence." (Pausanias *4.33.3*) Perhaps delicacy forbids Pausanias to mention that these square blocks of stone called "Herms," standing about in the open street, often had a head and the male genitalia.

As Hermes was a god of roads and travelers, these were supposed to reassure travelers of his power or strength to keep away the forces that might cause harm to them.

However, some statues of Hermes, which usually were placed in some other god's temple, were very beautiful; Praxiteles' Hermes holding the Infant Dionysus, discovered in the 1800s in the ruins of Hera's temple at Olympia, is the most famous of these.

Hermes also had, or shared, some temples. "Of the gods the people of Pheneos in Arcadia especially worship Hermes, in whose honor they celebrate the games called Hermaia; they have also a temple of Hermes, and a stone image, made by an Athenian, Eukheir the son of Euboulides. Behind the temple is the grave of Myrtilos, who was said to be the son of Hermes, and charioteer to Oinomaos." (Pausanias *8.14.10*)

Hermes and Aphrodite shared a large temple in the complex around the Temple of Hera at Samos which was built at the beginning of the 6th century BCE.

11. B. Temple of Mercury

The **Aedes** of Mercury was dedicated by a centurion, M. Plaetorius, to whom the people had given this honor in 495 BCE on the Ides of May. This later became the date of the **Mercuralia**, a festival of the merchants (Livy *II.21.7, 27.5-6*). On this day the merchants sprinkled their heads and their merchandise with water from Mercury's well near the Porta Capena. The temple was on the slope of the Aventine Hill near its southeast end above and facing the Circus Maximus. (Ovid, *Fasti V, 669*). This was a fitting place to worship a god of trade and swiftness, since it was a major center of commerce as well as a racetrack. As it stood between the plebeian stronghold on the Aventine and the patrician center on the Palatine, it also bridged the major parts of Roman society.

Maia seems also to have shared this temple with her son (Macrobius, *Saturnalia. I. 12.19*; Martial *VII 74.5*). If, as many believe, this temple is represented on a coin of Marcus Aurelius, it had a podium of three steps, on which stood four herms in place of columns, supporting an architrave, and above this what looks like a curved pediment with animals and attributes of the god. The statue of Mercury stood between the herms. No traces of this temple, which was standing in the fourth century, have been found.

The ruins of great Roman temples to Mercury have also been found in Baalbek in Lebanon. These temples, however, are but a single aspect of a vast complex. Baalbek (about which we shall have more to say later) is unequaled for boldness of concept and skill in utilizing Herculean masonry.

12. A. Temples of Hephaestus In Athens

The Temple of Hephaestus and Athena in Athens, (the **Hephaesteum**, also known as the Theseum), still stands. This most complete extant example of a Doric temple was built in 449 BCE on a hill close to the Agora at the foot of the Acropolis. It was designed by Ictinus, co-designer together with Kallikrates of the Athenian Parthenon, and has been preserved almost intact as a result of having been made into the Christian Church of St George (a major 3rd century Christian martyr who was possibly a soldier of the Roman Empire,) in the 7th century CE. As might have been expected, the survival of the exterior came at the cost of the ancient interior, whose original attributes were considered by no means suitable to a Christian church. The festival "Chalceia" on the 30th day of the month **Pyanopsion** honored Hephaestus and Athena **Ergane** (protectress of craftsman and artisans).

12. B. Temple of Vulcan

The Volcanal, sometimes called 'The Temple of Vulcan,' was one of the most ancient religious centers of Rome, but it was an altar or shrine at the left side of the Rostra in the Roman Forum at the foot of the slope of the Capitoline Hill rather than an actual temple. The Volcanal had a huge lotus tree, which was said to have been planted when it was first built. A special priest, the **Flamen Volcanalis**, took care of his cult. (And, it is to be hoped, the tree. When such plants died, there could be major repercussions). Here a tablet has been found documenting a gift by Augustus Caesar to the god Vulcan in 9 BCE.

There were two major festivals in Vulcan's honor: the **Tubilustrium** on May 23, and the **Vulcanalia**, dating back to the ancient Roman kingdom, which was celebrated on August 23 (the first day of Virgo), perhaps as a way of asking Vulcan's protection during the hot Mediterranean summer, which is the period of highest risk of fire. On the banks of the river Tiber, fires were lighted on which living fish were sacrificed (a nasty practice, reminiscent of what happens to lobsters in the present day). In 215 BCE, Vulcan's temple on the Circus Flaminius was inaugurated.

Vulcan was said to have fathered Servius Tullius, one of the kings of Rome, who because of his parentage was supposedly able to cause fire to descend on his enemies. (There is no evidence that he actually did so, and his messy and tragic end brought no retribution from his supposed parent).[18]

SECTION III. GREAT EARTH GODS

1. A. Temple of Demeter

About 22 km. east of Athens lies one of the most important sacred spots of antiquity, the sanctuary of Eleusis, dedicated to Demeter and her daughter Persephone. This impressive site of the Eleusinian Mysteries, which boasts large porticoes, a rectangular fountain, arches, public and private buildings, hot springs, inns and baths for the pilgrims, begins at the external yard where the Sacred Way from Athens ended.

In the center of the yard is an area sacred to Artemis and Poseidon, and the ancient well where women danced in honor of Demeter and Persephone. The great **Propylaia**, or entranceway, leads to the sanctuary, the **Prytaneum**, the sacred dwelling of Kirykos, and the underground cisterns. As has been mentioned, nearby is the **Plutonion**, the small temple of Pluto Hades, and in the cavity of the rock, the chasm through which the god of the underworld led Persephone back to earth.

The internal Sacred Way leads to wide stairs, where an amphitheatrical formation of the space implies that the secret mysteries were held there. Further along the Sacred Way is the famous Eleusinian Telesterio, which held 3,000 spectators for the Mysteries and contains a Palace in the center of the hall. Unlike the rest of Greece, where religion was open to all, at Eleusis the mysteries were controlled by a closed group of initiates who had sworn to uphold the strict confidentiality of the secret rites.

From various writers we get tantalizing glimpses into the Mysteries, which celebrated the march of the seasons, the cycle of life. The initiates evidently held up an ear of corn as a symbol of earth's boundless fertility and inspired the worshippers to see the cycle of rebirth in the branching ears, and individual lives in the rows of kernels, which at planting time are hidden away in the soil and reborn in each cycle, just as Persephone, queen of the dead, enters the underworld each year and emerges again, bringing springtime and new life on earth.

Diodorus Siculus recounts some myths bearing on the Mysteries. Stressing that it is not lawful for any but the initiated to hear about the mysteries, he indicates that Zeus instructed one Iasion in the rites, which had been celebrated on the island of Samothrace from ancient times. This Iasion is a troublesome figure, sometimes portrayed as a mortal lover of Demeter whom Zeus struck dead with a thunderbolt. Some say he was a minor agricultural god who founded the Kabeirian Mysteries of Samothrace to honor Demeter, Persephone, Hecate and the Kabeiroi. The Mystery cult evidently expanded on Iasion's various biographies and represented him as a springtime consort of Demeter, who returned to the upper world every spring in the company of Demeter's daughter Persephone.

Diodorus says (*V, 48, 49*) that although the details of the initiatory rite are closely guarded and are communicated to the initiates alone, the story of how these gods appear to mankind and bring unexpected aid to those initiates of theirs who call upon them in the midst of perils is very well-known. The claim is also made that men who have taken part in the mysteries become more pious, more just, and better in every respect than they were before. (This could lead us to wish that more people had taken part). The most famous of the ancient heroes and of the demigods were eager to take part in the initiatory rite; and in fact Jason, Heracles and Orpheus were said after their initiation to have attained success in the campaigns they undertook, because the gods of Eleusis appeared to them. (If this is the Orpheus who married Eurydice, not all his undertakings were successful). [19]

The Demetria, a Greek festival in honor of Demeter, was held at seed-time for ten days. All we know about this celebration is the intriguing fact that the men who took part in it lashed one another with whips of bark, while the women made lewd jokes. (Perhaps this was a way of relaxing from the strain of keeping the secret of the Mysteries, as secret-keeping is not very compatible with human nature.)

1. B. Temple of Ceres

Ceres was associated with a special cult of the ancient Italic goddess Tellus, who personified the Earth. They shared an ancient feast day on December 13, marking the end of the sowing season. The **Feriae Sementivae**, associated with the protection of seeded crops, honored both goddesses in the latter half of January. The festival of Tellus, the **Fordicicia**, was celebrated on April 15. The great festival of Ceres, the **Cerealia** (from which comes the modern word cereal) occurred on April 19, only four days later, an interval of time often used by the Romans to separate related festivals (Spaeth, *The Roman Goddess Ceres*, 5). Tellus was often mentioned alongside Ceres in early Roman funeral sacrifices, but Ceres slowly eclipsed Tellus and began to be associated directly with the Earth herself.

The Temple of Ceres dedicated in 494 BCE on the Aventine Hill, where she was worshipped together with Liber and Libera, represented a distinctly Italic cult, although similarities between her worship and that of Demeter would grow as time passed. This Triad's temple directly faced the Circus Maximus and stood outside the **pomerium**, the sacred boundary of the city. Since only native Roman cults were allowed inside the **pomerium**, this may mark the Triad as being perceived as somehow foreign, or more probably as representative of the plebeians, or ordinary Roman citizens, since this Aventine Triad, allegedly created as the result of a consultation of the Sibylline Books, was the plebeian counterpart of the Capitoline Triad of Jupiter, Juno, and Minerva. Perhaps this was natural, as Ceres, Liber and Libera were concerned with agriculture much more than with statecraft, which occupied a great part of the patrician, or upper, class's attention. However that may have been, the temple on the Aventine became a focal point for plebeian class-consciousness and political organization in the early Republic.

The plebeian magistrates, the tribunes and aediles, were closely associated with Ceres, and the aediles, who served as priests in the Aventine Triad's cult, stored the archives of the decrees of the Roman Senate and of the **Concilium Plebes** in her temple. Fines levied by plebeian aediles were frequently presented to the goddess as gifts. "And likewise games were held and golden paterae placed at the temple of Ceres by the plebeian aediles L. Aelius Paetus and C Fulvius Curvus with the money from fines that they had collected from those convicted of [illegally] using public pasture." (Livy *10.23.13*)

The perilous office of the tribune of the plebs was protected by Ceres directly. These tribunes held a number of important powers, such as the right to protect plebs from patrician magistrates, and the right to impede the action of any patrician magistrate. These two rights helped make the plebeian tribune one of the strongest (and most dangerous) offices in the entire Roman government. Anyone who harmed a plebeian tribune could be killed with impunity, and his goods consecrated to Ceres. (The developments concerning Ceres and her worshippers in the early Roman Republic were of course related to a major power squabble that began at the establishment of that republic. Patricians claimed to be descended from the gods, and on that score to be the only ones suitable to give sacrifices, as the gods, evidently being rather shortsighted, only recognized their own relatives. Since all officials had to be priests as well as politicians, these godly descendants were trying to hold on to all the offices in the new **res publica**).

The new Triadic cult melded with the much older cult of Ceres alone and formally assumed all of its functions, with a new emphasis on protecting the urban grain supply as well as the plebeians.

Festivals - Ambarvalia and Dea Dia

All this blending of cults and constant re-invention of various forms of the nurturing Earth Mother produces major headaches for the modern researcher, whose troubles are not lessened by contemplation of the **Ambarvalia**, a very important agriculture-related festival held in May, whose peculiar name means "going around the fields." The Ambarvalia, as we might expect, involved a circumambulation, a procession around the cultivated lands of the city during which prayers were said and lustrations, sacrifices designed to ensure that all evil was excluded from within the circle that had been circumambulated, were offered. May was the most crucial month for the crops in Rome, and thus such purification ceremonies were performed in order to guarantee a healthy harvest. Ceres as Earth Mother was celebrated by women in secret rituals at this festival, to which references are found in various writings including those of Strabo (c. 64 BCE-24 CE), Festus (c. late second century CE), and in Macrobius' *Saturnalia.7* (c. 400 CE). In addition, Cato (234-149 BCE), Vergil (70-19 BCE), and Tibullus (48-19 BCE) speak of private Ambarvalia ceremonies in which rites were observed very similar to those performed during the public festival. Therefore, from very early Roman literature there are various recorded testimonies to the continuance of the Ambarvalia ceremony over a prolonged period. By the time of Augustus' reign it had become impossible to circumambulate physically the ever-increasing boundaries around Rome, and thus the ceremonies and sacrifices were made at certain circumscribed locations.

At the sacred grove on Via Campana, the festival of Dea Dia was also celebrated by the Arval Brethren,[20] and although this feast was movable, its customary date was May 29. Because of the similarities between this festival and that of Ambarvalia, it has been suggested that these were one and the same festivals. In the famous **Carmen Arvale** (*Arval Hymn*) recited during the festival of Dea Dia, the Lares (as gods of the soil), Semones (god of seed and abundance) and Mars are petitioned in order to protect the land and harvest. Records concerning Dea Dia show that she had characteristics similar to those of Ceres, but the **Carmen Arvale** contains no direct reference to Dea Dia, being concerned with asking the protection of Mars, here shown in his very ancient persona as a defender of crops. The Arval Brethren at the end of the hymn call upon both the combative and defensive character of Mars. Cato, in a ritual to be performed during a private Ambarvalia ceremony proposes a prayer to be recited, in which Mars is invoked in similar terms to that found in the hymn of the Arval Brethren. Cato's prayer calls on Mars to combat demons that threaten the crops. "Drive back, and cast out the visible and invisible ailments, calamities and disasters . . . so that the wheat, vines, and young shoots increase and come to a good end . . ."

Such a lustration ceremony had no doubt been observed since the origins of Rome, whereby the boundary of the cultivated land was marked off from that of the wilderness, the sacred from the profane. This boundary-line was itself eventually to become sacred, marked by a procession, prayers and sacrifice, usually in May, when crops were vulnerable to disease.

Temple of Cybele

As we have seen, the patricians were suspected of importing the cult of Magna Mater, or Cybele, explicitly so that their social class would have a goddess that served some of the functions that Ceres served for the plebeians. As a result, there was sharp antagonism between the two cults, who became rivals separated by the social classes they served. The cult of Cybele was imported from Asia Minor in 204 BCE, and welcomed into the city by a *vir optimus*, or best man, selected from one of the most distinguished patrician families. The matrons that escorted the goddess on the road from Ostia to Rome were entirely drawn from the patrician class. After the completion of Magna Mater's temple on the Palatine in 191 BCE, games were established in her honor during which patricians received special privileges and patrician families held banquets. Magna Mater's games, the **Ludi Megalenses**, directly preceded the **Cerealia** and were celebrated by the curule aediles, who were drawn largely from the patrician class. The Palatine itself was a district largely associated with the patricians, and the temple of Ceres, Liber, and Libera on the Aventine directly faced the temple of Magna Mater that stood there.

Not to be outdone, the plebeians instituted a new festival, called the **ieinium Cereris**, in same year in which the temple of Magna Mater was dedicated. The festival lasted nine days and was originally held every five years, though it was held every year beginning on October 4 by the time of Augustus. This festival in which women fasted and offered the first wheat harvest to Ceres, culminated with rites celebrated on the 19th. It is not surprising that on the evening of the 19th, plebeian families invited each other to dinner parties where the ladies broke their fast with a vengeance.

2. A. Temple of Dionysus
The Temple and the Theater of Dionysus at Athens

Just below one bluff of the Athenian Acropolis stands the Temple of Dionysus, and next to it, as anyone conversant with Greek history well knows, the Theater of Dionysus, which took on its definitive form at the end of the 4th century BCE when it was renovated by Likourgos, an archon of Athens who luckily was also an art lover with good architectural taste. Most of the great Greek plays were initially written to be performed at the important feast of Dionysus, held in the spring when the leaves begin to reappear on the vine. Thus this theater was a wellspring of dramatic art in which tragedies of Aeschylus, Sophocles, and Euripides, as well as the comedies of Aristophanes and Menandros, were presented for the first time. Writers, actors, spectators were regarded as sacred servants of Dionysus during the festival. (Whether the beverage of the god played a prominent part in their dramatic performances and audience response to them we will not ask).

2. B a. Temple of Liber

We have said that the temple erected in 494 BCE on the Aventine hill was devoted to the Aventine Triad, Ceres, Liber, and Libera. Liber's festival, which he shared with his counterpart deity Libera, was called the Liberalia and celebrated on March 17. A major part of the festival featured old women called **sacerdotes Liberi** wearing crowns of ivy selling honey cakes in the street. The cakes were fried on portable hearths, and a part of each cake bought was offered to Liber in the name of the buyer. Young men who had reached seventeen years of age also gained the right to wear man's clothing, the *toga* **uirilis** or **liber,** during this festival.

Liber also shared a temple with Hercules (Heracles), erected on the Quirinal Hill by the emperor Septimius Severus. That temple was the second largest ever built in Rome, with columns over 21 meters high and a central square that covered 13,000 square meters. These two gods were paired and presented with the new cult because they were the patron gods of the emperor's birthplace at Leptis Magna in North Africa.

2. B b. Temple of Bacchus

Bacchus was another matter. His festival, also on March 16 and 17, may have overwhelmed the older and quieter celebration. As we have seen, the **Bacchanalia**, orgies in honor of Dionysus, were introduced in Rome around 200 BCE and became so appalling that in 186 BCE the Roman Senate made an attempt to eradicate them, which merely succeeded in driving them underground.

The Temple of Bacchus at Baalbek, which many historians consider the best-preserved Roman temple of its size, is part of Baalbek's immense semiruins. It has nineteen unfluted Corinthian columns still standing from its original forty-two and well-preserved exterior walls. The approach to the **cella** or worship room is as grand as it is huge. The inner side walls of the nave are divided into bays by projected Corinthian half-columns to produce a series of superimposed niches, round-headed below and shaped into pediments above where originally there were statues.

Section IV Temples and Festivals of Uniquely Roman Deities

1. Shrine to the Genius of the Roman People

Near the temple of Concord in the Roman Forum stood a shrine dedicated to the Genius of the Roman people, mentioned twice in connection with prodigies in the years 43 and 32 BCE (Cassius Dio *XLVII 2. 3; L 8.2*) and on an inscription found in the Roman Forum between the **Clivus Capitolinus** and the **Basilica Julia**. Sacrifices were offered on October 9 to the **Genius populi Romani, Felicitas** and **Venus Victrix in Capitolio**, and therefore there was probably a shrine or altar on the Capitol also, which was dedicated to the Genius or perhaps, considering the Roman fondness for groups of three, to this triad.

2. Temple of Janus

On the north side of the forum stood a shrine of Janus, usually referred to simply as **Ianus Geminus** or **Ianus Quirinus**. (Just as scholars get troublesome old Quirinus, who keeps popping up as a very early Roman deity, paired with Mars, here he is teaming up with Janus). It was also called **Geminae Belli Portae**, (twin gates of war). As we might expect, scholars have varying views concerning this edifice, but matters here are even more confused than usual. Shrine that it was, whether it was an enclosure with an altar and a pair of gates at each end, or some other structure, it seems doubtful that it was a temple in the usual sense. When it was erected is another obscure point. According to one story (Macrobius, *Saturnalia I.9. 17-18)*, it was present at the founding of Rome when Titus Tatius and his Sabines, just about to dispense with Romulus and his girl-stealing followers[21] before they got their city really going, were stopped and driven back by floods of hot water which Janus helpfully poured forth from his holy place at the base of the Viminal Hill right through the gate of the city. Because of this, the gate was called the **Porta Ianualis** and apparently identified or confused with the shrine. A variant of this legend made the erection of the shrine a result of this intervention of the god (Ovid *Fasti I. 263-276)*. Another tradition was that Romulus and Tatius built the temple (or whatever it was) as a sign of the union of the two communities and still another that it was erected by King Numa as an indicator of the status quo, (Livy *I. 19*) in order that when open it might indicate that Rome was at war, and when closed that she was at peace. This became the accepted mission of the shrine, and the doors must have gotten rather squeaky with disuse, since after the reign of Numa, who died in 673 BCE, its doors were next closed in 235 BCE after the first Punic War. The next hiatus came in 30 BCE after the battle of Actium, and Augustus had occasion (or time) to close the gates only twice more. Thanks to his **Pax Augusta**, which morphed into the **Pax Romana**, they were closed at more frequent intervals down to the fifth century.

Artist's concept of the Shrine of Janus

There is no mention of any rebuilding of this uncertain structure, and therefore it was probably never moved from its original site, which, scholars examining the traditions for once generally agree, must have been near the point where the **Argiletum** entered the forum close to the **curia**, or Senate House. Excavations of its supposed site between the **curia** and the west end of the **Basilica Aemilia**, however, have as yet shown hardly any space for even so small a building as Procopius and various coins tell us it was: a small rectangular structure of bronze, with two side walls and double doors at each end. The walls, not as high as the doors, had grating on top. These gratings and the arches over the doors supported an entablature extending all around the building, but there was no roof. The ancient bronze statue of the two-faced god stood in the centre of what was evidently no temple in the ordinary sense but a passage (**ianus**). No traces of the structure have ever been found, and there is no reference to it after Procopius.

Thus we bring to a close our tour of the labor, time, and vast amounts of capital expended in the worship of the Greek and Roman deities. The ancients developed their artistic talents, and their creative imaginations, in the invention and the worship of supernatural beings who, they hoped, would have enough interest in mankind and enough control of natural phenomena to help them in their great struggle not only to survive and prosper, but also to beautify and enrich the world around them.

NOTES:

1. See Appendix I

2. The nine Muses, the Greek goddesses who inspire and preside over the arts and sciences, were Calliope: eloquence & heroic poetry; Clio: history, Erato: lyric & amatory poetry; Euterpe: music; Melpomene: tragedy: Polyhymnia: lyric poetry; Terpsichore: dance & choral song: Thalia: comedy; and Urania: astronomy.

3. The seven hills upon which Rome was built were the Capitoline, the Palatine, the Aventine, the Caelian, the Quirinal, the Viminal, and the Esquiline.

4. Around 390 BC tribes of Gauls began to move down from northern Italy into Etruria and to wage war on the Romans. These barbarians were truly worthy of the name, being big, untamed, and unwashed. In battle they had little discipline, but men of their size fighting like circle saws didn't seem to need it. At the river Allia they not only defeated the Romans, but sent them flying back into the city without even closing the gates. The Romans didn't stop running until they reached the fortified citadel on the Capitoline Hill. Here they were besieged by the Gauls, who attempted to creep up the hill during the night. Juno's sacred geese, who were among those present, disapproved of these intruders and cackled loud enough to awake Marcus Manlius Capitolinus, who called the alarm to his fellows and wasted no time toppling the Gauls from the hill. According to legend, he did not remain a hero for long, however, as he defended plebeian debtors from harsh patrician creditors, and the following year was impeached for high treason and thrown from the Tarpeian Rock by the tribunes. The geese, however, continued to be considered heroes by all.

5. According to one myth Medusa, a beautiful maiden whose hair was her chief glory, had the unmitigated gall to claim she was more beautiful than Athena. Unfortunately, Athena heard this modest little statement, and suddenly Medusa's shining locks became hissing snakes. This

soured her outlook on life considerably, and she became a Gorgon, a cruel monster of so frightening an aspect that no living thing could behold her without being turned into stone. All around the cavern where she now dwelt might be seen the rigid figures of unfortunate men and animals that had happened to catch a glimpse of her. The hero Perseus, fortified with a bit of help from Athena and Hermes, the former of whom lent him her shield and the latter his winged shoes, sneaked up on Medusa while she slept. (He may have been heroic, but he wasn't stupid). Guided by her image reflected in Athena's shining shield, he cut off her head and then, at a loss as to what to do with it, presented it to Athena, who fixed it in the middle of her aegis. Some ancient poets with a ghastly love of horror claim that there were three Gorgons, and of them only Medusa was mortal.

6 Circe and Medea, two devotees of the goddess Hecate, were the two best-known great sorceresses of the ancient world. They were young and beautiful, which stands to reason, since a female of such great powers would be unlikely go around as an old hag. Medea was the daughter of King Aeetes of Colchis, and the granddaughter of Helios, the sun god. She fell in love with the adventurer Jason and helped him steal the Golden Fleece from her father. A firm believer in the "all for love" philosophy and a bit short on moral fiber, Medea cut her younger brother Absyrtis in pieces to distract her father from pursuing her and her lover as they fled, then in a similar manner dispatched Pelias, the king of Iolcus who had usurped the throne belonging to Jason's father by a singularly underhanded method, to his exceedingly questionable eternal reward. Having made Iolcus too hot to hold them, Jason and Medea fled to Corinth, where, two offspring later, Jason was harebrained enough to plan to desert Medea and marry the daughter of Creon King of Corinth. This bit of social climbing on his part not only brought his fiancee a fiery death, but caused Medea to kill her two children to punish him. Medea borrowed her grandfather Helios' chariot, fittingly drawn by winged dragons, and fled to Athens, where she married Aegeus, the old king of Athens, and bore him a son, Medus. She tried to trick old Aegeus into poisoning his son Theseus. When this didn't work, she took her son and fled again, disappearing, to everyone's intense relief, from Greek literature.

Circe lived in the Mediterranean on an island named Aeaea. If this name sounds like a scream, it should. Circe whiled away her duller hours by turning any men who came her way into beasts–the four-footed kind. The poor fellows retained their reason but had inadequate voices to complain about their misfortunes. Anyone approaching the island too closely could hear the roars, oinks, and other assorted noises made by Circe's unwilling guests. At one point Picus, grandfather of King Latinus whom Aeneas met in Italy, wed Circe. After a pleasant honeymoon, Circe in a fit of pique turned Picus into a woodpecker.

7   Camilla was an Italian princess whose father Metabus had been such a cruel king that his people, the Volscians, had risen against him. He had fled for his life carrying his tiny daughter in his arms. When he reached the flooding river Amasenus, he knew that the Volscians were not far behind him and that he could not swim across the river carrying the baby. He wrapped Camilla carefully in the bark of a cork oak tree and tied her to a huge battle spear of oak. As he prepared to throw the spear, he prayed to the forest goddess Diana to protect the child and promised that she would be the servant of the goddess if she survived. The spear landed safely on the other side of the river, and Metabus swam across the water and escaped the pursuit with his little daughter.

While he lived the rest of his life as a shepherd in the forest, Metabus taught Camilla to worship Diana and to hunt with darts and slingshots. As Camilla grew older, she advanced to the weapons of war, which she used with appalling effectiveness. When the war between Aeneas the Trojan and the Italian prince Turnus began, Camilla, surrounded by a bodyguard of maiden warriors, joined Turnus and led the cavalry of the Volscians into battle. The Trojans were amazed by her beauty and grace, but they soon learned that she was dangerous. She killed many men in battle before she was killed by the Etruscan Arruns. The followers of Diana, who were incensed by her death, followed Arruns into a deserted valley and killed him.

8   The Minotaur, half man and half bull, was the result of a bizarre love affair between Minos' queen Pasiphae and a beautiful white bull that Poseidon had given Minos. When Minos refused to sacrifice the bull to Poseidon, the god took a leaf from Aphrodite's book and made the queen fall in love with it. When her offspring, the huge and carnivorous Minotaur, was born, Minos kept it in the Labyrinth, a giant maze, built for him by the Athenian Daedalus. Meanwhile Minos' son Androgeos went to Athens and was killed there, according to some stories by jealous rivals after he had won the Panathenaic games, according to others by the Marathonian bull that King Aegeus of Athens had sent him to fight. However the death of his heir came about, King Minos

blamed Athens as a whole and King Aegeus in particular. The seething king of Crete besieged Athens, and only withdrew after the city agreed to send a tribute of seven young men and seven maidens to Crete every nine years. These hapless youngsters were placed in the Labyrinth and eventually discovered and devoured by the Minotaur. All this nastiness came to an abrupt end when Ariadne, as noted in the Aphrodite section, fell in love with Theseus, crown prince of Athens and part of the latest shipment of sacrifices, and gave him a thread to use to find his way through the Labyrinth and a sword to deal with the Minotaur. (Some myths omit the sword and credit Theseus with twisting the Minotaur's head and breaking its neck, a feat that would definitely rank him as Chief Wrestler of Greece). He then fled, taking Ariadne, who felt that her father might be less than pleased with her, along and promising to wed her. When their ship paused for a brief rest on the island of Naxos, the ungrateful prince sneaked off and left her behind.

9   Eros/Cupid (also called Amor) is a troublesome rascal in more ways than one. In later mythology, Eros is the offspring of Aphrodite and Ares, but there are many varying stories concerning his parentage. In the *Theogony*, Hesiod mentions Eros as being an attendant of Aphrodite, but not her son. He was worshiped as a fertility god, believed to be a contemporary of the primeval Chaos (a state of affairs he was destined to bring on mortals again and again), which makes him one of the oldest gods. In the Dionysian Mysteries Eros is referred to as "protagonus", the first born. Aristophanes (*The Birds*) says that he was born from Erebus and Nyx (Night). Some early legends of Eros say that he was responsible for the embraces of Ouranus (Heaven or Sky) and Gaia (Earth), which as we know produced a variety of living things.

Eros is usually depicted as a young winged boy attired chiefly in a ribbon and the quiver of the arrows that wreaked such havoc on gods and men. His arrows came in two types: golden with dove feathers which aroused love, or leaden arrows which had owl feathers that caused indifference, and he employed them with devastating effectiveness. He was charming and very beautiful, but, like his mother, totally unscrupulous, and dangerous to all around him. Once, while he was busy making as much mischief as he possibly could, (which was a great deal) he himself fell in love. As usual, Eros was at his mother's side assisting her in all her godly (or ungodly) affairs. Aphrodite had become jealous of a beautiful young woman named Psyche, and asked Eros to shoot his arrow into the girl's heart and make her fall in love with the ugliest man on earth. He agreed to carry out his mother's wishes, but on seeing her beauty, he became as clumsy as the mortals he was always bedeviling and wounded himself with a golden arrow, which caused him to fall deeply in love with Psyche himself. He would visit her every night, but, having no doubt as to what Aphrodite's reaction to his little romance would be, he made himself invisible and told Psyche never to light her chamber or attempt to see him. Psyche fell in love with Eros even though she could not see him, but one night curiosity overcame her. She concealed a lamp, which she lit while Eros slept. As she bent in awe at her lover, a drop of hot oil spilt from the lamp, awakening the god. Angered by her lack of trust Eros fled, and the distraught Psyche roamed the earth trying in vain to find her lover. In the end Zeus took pity and, stifling the protests of Venus, reunited them and gave his consent for them to marry.

10 The "Orphic Hymns", a collection of about eighty short poems of praise to various divinities, were used in ritual and sacred practice for almost one thousand years, from 300 BC to AD 500 in Thrace, Phrygia, Anatolia and the rest of what we now call Asia Minor, as well as the Greek mainland and islands. They take their name from Orpheus, the famous and probably legendary poet and musician who is credited with founding the Orphic religion, one of the major belief systems of the archaic Hellenistic world.

Each of the hymns is headed by "the fumigation of aromatics" which usually includes a short description of the herbs or substances used as a means of calling on the deity. After the gods might be presumed to be sniffing and hopefully listening, hymns were chanted by groups in sacred circles to invoke particular deities.

11 Pietas -- the Roman chief virtue, which was tri-fold; loyalty to the gods, one's family, and one's country were necessary to achieve it. Like Peace and other Roman values, pietas was personified and received a temple in its honor in 181 BCE.

12 The curious treatment of the bean may relate to the bizarre belief that the Doxographists say Pythagoras learned from Zaratus of Chaldea. "Zaratas forbade men to eat beans because he said that at the beginning and composition of all things when the earth was still a whole, the bean arose. And he says that the proof of this is that if one chews a bean to a pulp and exposes it to the sun for a certain time (for the sun will affect it quickly), it gives out the odor of human seed. And he says that there is another and clearer proof: if when a bean is in flower we were

to take the bean and its flower, and putting it into a pitcher moisten it and then bury it in the earth, and after a few days dig it up again, we should see in the first place that it had the form of a womb, and examining it closely we should find the head of a child growing with it." Doxographists, Hippolytus. *Philosophumena;* Dox. *555: p.154*

Evidently this curious bit of legume prejudice was widespread: the Flamen Dialis of Rome was forbidden to eat beans, and according to Herodotus and Plutarch, so were the priests of Egypt. (*Herodotus II, 37*; Plutarch *Moralia: De Iside et Osiride*)

13 When the vulgar nouveau riche Trimalchio entertains his banquet guests by having his business announcements read, they include the pleasant tidbit that he has had a slave crucified for cursing his Genius (Petronius, *Satyricon, Trimalchio's Banquet, VIII, 53*). Later during the same unique meal, he is beseeched to forgive his wife's temper in the name of his good Genius. *(Satyricon, Trimalchio's Banquet, X, 75)*. Pliny the Younger, when writing to Emperor Trajan of his tussles with the Christians, says that one test he applied in checking for Christianity was to compel the suspect to honor a small statue of the emperor, and his Genius, with wine and incense. (Of course, Pliny was not eager to be hard on the Christians, hoping, as he ingeniously told Trajan, that by kindness and patience they could be won back to the 'true faith.') (Pliny, *Letters, X, 96*)

14 The list of the Seven Wonders of the Ancient World was compiled around the second century BCE. The first reference to the idea is found in Herodotus in the 5th century BCE.

1. The Pyramids of Egypt (which are numerous) usually contribute to this list the three pyramids at Giza, outside modern Cairo. The largest pyramid, built by Khufu (Cheops), a king of the fourth dynasty, had an original estimated height of 482 ft (now, after weather and marauders have had their way, approximately 450 ft). The base has sides 755 ft long. It contains 2,300,000 blocks; the average weight of each is 2.5 tons. Estimated date of completion is 2680 BC. Of all the Ancient Wonders on this list, the pyramids alone survive.

2. The Hanging Gardens of Babylon were supposedly built by Nebuchadnezzar around 600 BC to please his queen, Amuhia, but they are also associated with the mythical Assyrian queen, Semiramis. Archeologists surmise that the gardens were laid out atop a vaulted building, with provisions for raising water. The terraces were said to rise from 75 to 300 ft.

3. The Statue of Zeus at Olympia was made of gold and ivory by the Greek sculptor Pheidias in the 5th century BC. Reputed to be 40 ft high, the statue has been lost without a trace, except for reproductions on coins. (During periods of upheaval, artifacts made of precious materials have a way of disappearing).

4. The Temple of Artemis at Ephesus built in its greatest form about 350 BC in honor of a non-Hellenic goddess who later became identified with the Greek goddess of the same name. The temple, with Ionic columns 60 ft high, was destroyed by invading Goths in AD 262.

5. The Mausoleum at Halicarnassus was erected by Queen Artemisia in memory of her husband, King Mausolus of Caria in Asia Minor, who died in 353 BC. Some remains of the structure are in the British Museum. This shrine is the source of the modern word "mausoleum."

6. The Colossus at Rhodes was a bronze statue of Helios (Apollo), about 105 ft high. The sculptor Chares reputedly labored for 12 years before completing it in 280 BC, only to have it destroyed during an earthquake in 224 B.C.

7. The Pharos (Lighthouse) of Alexandria was built by Sostratus of Cnidus during the 3rd century BC on the island of Pharos off the coast of Egypt. An earthquake got it also but it lasted until the 13th century of our era.

15 The Roman system of dating always makes one wonder how they managed to conquer the world without outside help. To find the date, they counted backward (counting both beginning and ending day) from the nearest of three named days of the month-- the Kalends, the Nones, and the Ides. The Kalends, which gives us our word Calendar, was the first day of each month. In March, May, July, and October, the Ides fell on the 15th day, making the Nones, which was nine days before the Ides, fall on the 7th. In all other months, the Ides was the 13th day and the Nones the 5th.

16 Pontifex Maximus - The head or high priest of the ancient Roman College of Priests. During the Roman Republic, the Pontifex Maximus was elected by the Comitia Tributa and served for life. The main task of the whole body of priests was to advise the government officials so that the *pax deorum*, or 'peace with the gods' might be maintained. To do this they carefully observed and interpreted the omens they observed in natural phenomena such as the flight of birds. The pontifex maximus collected and recorded the omens (*annales maximi*) and the events that followed them. He also controlled the calendar, oversaw other priests,

the Vestal Virgins, and funerals. This, the most important position in classical Roman religion, gradually became more politicized, and under Augustus Caesar became part of the Emperor's duties.

17 Iphigenia, like so many mythological figures, has multiple biographies. The simplest states that she was the daughter of King Agamemnon of Mycenae and his wife Clytemnestra. When Agamemnon, commander of the Greek army preparing to invade Troy, assembled his fleet at the little port of Aulis, he or one of his men offended Artemis, probably by killing one of her sacred animals. She promptly sent a contrary wind to prevent any sailing, and the crafty old priest Calchas said that Agamemnon's daughter must be sacrificed to the goddess if the fleet were ever to sail. Agamemnon, grieving but full of that "my country right or wrong" sentiment that does so much damage in the annals of history, sent for his daughter under the pretence that she was to be married to Achilles. Clytemnestra, overjoyed at this prospect, brought her daughter and loads of wedding clothes to Aulis. She was appalled when she learned the true plan, and Achilles, whose name had been employed in a way he considered dishonorable, to say the least, declared that he would defend the maiden. In this episode, Achilles was overborne, and Iphigenia was sacrificed. The Greeks sailed for Troy, leaving Clytemnestra with the ten years of the war to plan a fitting homecoming for Agamemnon, which she accomplished with the help of a sword (or some same, with a battleaxe), on his return from Troy.

According to one version, Iphigenia was never slain but a deer was put in her place at the altar and Iphigenia was taken by Artemis to Tauria where she became Artemis' priestess only to be taken back to Greece, perhaps Bauronia, by her brother Orestes after he avenged his father's death by slaying his mother. (The Greeks may not have invented dysfunctional families, but they certainly employed the concept in their literature).

18 Servius Tullius, legendary sixth king of Rome, gained the throne by the contrivance of Queen Tanaquil, wife of Rome's fifth king Tarquin Priscus, who fancied herself a great prophetess. Tullius, said to be the son of a household slave, was anointed as a young child to become king, after a spontaneous fire played about his head without burning him and he was proclaimed by Tanaquil to be destined to rule. (This story probably led to the legend that Vulcan was his father). He was then raised as a prince and married to the princess Tarquinia. He is credited with many achievements for Rome, among them protection of the poor, the formation of the Latin League and the first census.

Some of legislation was extremely distasteful to the upper class, and his person was evidently distasteful to his daughter Tullia. His reign of forty-four years was brought to a close in 535 BC by a conspiracy headed by his son-in-law Tarquinius Superbus and Tullia, his wife. After Tarquinius had killed him, Tullia drove her cart over her father's body, causing the unfortunate street in which this appalling deed took place ever after to bear the name of the "Vicus Sceleratus" (Street of Infamy).

19 Orpheus, the legendary founder of the Orphic religion and the most accomplished musician of the age, is said to have received from Apollo the lyre that Hermes invented and gave to his angry brother. The music of Orpheus could charm people, angry or not, wild beasts and even rocks and streams. The Greeks, who loved a good story no matter how outlandish, said that the oak trees growing along the coast of Thrace migrated there the better to hear the songs of Orpheus. When his beloved wife Eurydice died, Orpheus went to Hades with his lyre to get her back. Milton (*Il Penseroso*) says that he played so beautifully that he "drew iron tears down Pluto's cheek, and made Hell grant what love did seek." Although both Pluto and Persephone pitied Orpheus, Pluto was deliberately vague in the instructions for getting out of Hades, and Eurydice had to go back. Orpheus himself died after being set upon by a mob. One story claims that intoxicated followers of Dionysius tore the musician limb from limb. In another story, a mob of women angry because the musician, still in love with his long dead wife, had spurned their affection, stabbed Orpheus to death.

20 Arval Brethren (Fratres Arvales) was a body of priests in Rome similar to the Sabine priesthood of the Sodales Titii, both of whom offered annual sacrifices to the gods to guarantee good harvests. Roman legend held that Romulus originated the Arval Brethren as college of 12 priests, but archeologists have found no more than 9 names in the inscriptions at the same time. Appointed for life, even if exiled (a fate that often befell influential Romans) they did not lose their status.

The Arval Brethren conducted a festival in May in honor of the Dea Dia, a corn deity who was probably an aspect of Ceres. The master of the college selected the exact three days of the feast by an unknown method. The celebration started in Rome on the first day, was transferred to a sacred grove outside the city wall on the second day, and ended back in the city in the third day.

Their other duties included ritual thanksgivings and ambarvalia, the sacrifices connected to Roman boundaries. Before the sacrifice, the sacrificial animal was lead three times around a cornfield while a chorus of farmers and farm-servants danced and sang praises for Ceres and offered her libations of milk, honey and wine.

21 When Romulus was building the city of Rome, it suffered from a lack of marriageable females. Their bid to court the daughters of the Sabines, an Italian tribe who lived nearby, having been repulsed, the Romans proclaimed a festival and invited the Sabines to it. While the Sabines were watching some of the Romans in athletic endeavors, the others carried the girls off to hasty marriages. The Sabine men, understandably furious, were led by their king Titus Tatius, in a war on Romulus and his sneaky Romans. Titus Tatius delayed (or was delayed by Janus the two-faced god and his floodtide) just a little too long however, and the Sabine women, who had grown fond of their Roman husbands, rushed into the battle and begged both sides to make peace. So the war ended, and Romulus and Titus Tatius ruled together over the two peoples until Titus Tatius was killed in battle.

Appendix I

Julius Caesar, Marcus Tullius Cicero and many other educated Romans actually looked to philosophy for many of the comforts moderns tend to seek in religion. However, this did not keep them from practicing the state religion. Caesar was Pontifex Maximus; the last night of his life he spent in the Regia, the *domus publica* supplied by his office. We have no writings of Caesar which deal extensively with religion, but Cicero, who was an augur, one of the Roman priests to whom the will of the gods and the future were revealed by studying all aspects of the flight of birds, states *in De Divinatione (II 148-150)* that he is careful to keep the rituals, ceremonies, and customs of his ancestors, but to keep religion and superstition separated. Great attention was given to omens and portents in every aspect of Roman daily life because of their belief that everything in Nature was inhabited by *numina*, powers that manifested the divine will by means of natural phenomena which the pious Roman constantly sought to interpret. The function of the augurs, known as taking the auspices, was paramount in any Roman public or private undertaking, from architecture to war. The historian Livy says in *Book VI. 41* of his history: *auspiciis hanc urbem conditam esse, auspiciis bello ac pace domi militiaeque omnia geri, quis est qui ignoret?* ("Is there anyone who does not know that this city was founded, and that every move at home and elsewhere, in peace or in war, followed the taking of the auspices?"). Thus edifices and undertakings were "inaugurated." Cicero praises augury, which he himself practiced, while denigrating the Etruscan haruspices, who cut open sacrificial animals and examined their entrails for signs from the gods. This feeling of superiority may stem from the fact that the auspices did not pretend to foretell the future; they only told men what they should or should not do in the present instance, and were therefore seen as more practical.

In his book *De Natura Deorum*, which is an extensive study of what the various Greek and Roman philosophers said about the existence and functions of the gods, Cicero says that most thinkers believe the gods exist, and that this is the most probable view; one, in fact, to which nature leads us.(*De Natura Deorum Book I,1,2*) He admits that Pythagoras and others were doubtful about this, and that a few thinkers held there were no gods at all. Before he gives in exhaustive detail the positions of various schools of philosophy, he states his preference for the Academic philosophy, which long ago despaired of dogmatic certainty and settled for simple probability (Ibid. 5-14). He creates a conversation between Cotta, Velleius, and Balbus, who discuss varying views held by the major schools of thought about the origin, purpose, attitudes and attributes of the gods. Some believe the gods created the world and take an active interest in mankind; some believe they have human form; some believe they are merely cosmic forces which have no embodiment and no interest in anything earthly or human. Both Greeks and Romans seem to view the myths as simple literary and artistic conventions from earlier eras. Two important influences strengthened religion in the Romans, however. The first was their cardinal virtue *pietas*, which entwined the ancient gods and their rituals with its other two parts, the love of family and patriotism to the state. The second was the fact that the first Roman gods had been 'numina', formless powerful forces, and the idea of gods in human form came later through the influence of the Etruscans and Greeks; thus the Romans were able to smile at the myths and still reverence the gods.

Index

A

Acheron 28
Achilles 18, 39, 60, 122
Aeacus 28
Aedes 85, 87, 88, 93, 102
aediles 107, 109
aegis 35, 60, 116
Aeneas 5, 27, 33, 39, 49, 50, 51, 52, 53, 58, 62, 66, 72, 91, 100, 117
Aeneid 5, 24, 26, 27, 30, 51, 58, 61, 62, 66, 72, 73, 94
Aeolus 26, 27, 52
Aeschylus 60, 110, 133
Agamemnon 38, 39, 43, 44, 47, 96, 122
Agrippa 85, 86
Alba Longa 54, 87
Alcmena 21, 22
Amor -. *See* Eros, Cupid
Amphitrite 13, 25
Amphitryon 21, 22
Anchises 49
Apollodorus 64
Apophoreta 76
Arachne 35
Arcas 22
Areopagus 53, 100
Arethusa 30, 65
Argos 23, 81, 91

Argus 20, 58
Ariadne 49, 69, 71, 118
Aricia 98, 99
Arx 23, 83
Asclepius 38
Atalanta 48, 67
Athens 3, 14, 25, 36, 46, 49, 53, 64, 70, 75, 79, 80, 87, 90, 91, 95, 96, 99, 100, 101, 103, 105, 110, 116, 117, 118
augurs, augury, inauguration 18, 88, 125
Augustus Caesar 85, 93, 94, 101, 103, 108, 110, 113, 122
Avernus 31

B

Baalbek 103, 111
Bacchanalia 71, 111
beans 63, 119
Bellerophon 25
Briareos and other hundred-handed giants 5, 15
Brontes and other Cyclopes 5

C

Cacus 61
caduceus 55, 56, 58
Caesar, Julius 100, 124

127

Calchas 44, 122
Callisto 22, 43
Camenae. *See* Muses
Camilla 46, 117
Campus Martius 24, 85, 93, 101
Campus Sceleris 89
Capitoline Hill 19, 23, 36, 51, 61, 66, 73, 80, 81, 83, 91, 95, 100, 103, 107, 115
Cassandra 38
Cassius Dio 84, 93, 94, 112, 127
Castalia 37
Castor 47
Caucasus, Mount 60
Cerealia 106, 109
Ceyx 24
Chaos 4, 118
Charon 28
Chiron 7, 38
Chryses 39
Cicero, Marcus Tullius 5, 18, 76, 124, 125
Circe 44, 116, 117
Circus Flaminius 85, 104
Clymene 9
Clytemnestra 47, 122
Clytie 39
Cocytus 28
Colchis 49, 116
Constantine 33
Coronis 38
Crete 7, 15, 21, 49, 63, 64, 117, 118
Cupid 21, 52, 53, 118
Curetes 87
Cyclopes 5, 38, 43, 60, 61
Cynthus, Mount 96
Cythera 46, 99

D

Daedalus 117
Daphne 38
Dardanus 91
Delos 36, 87, 96
Delphi 14, 16, 37, 70, 87, 92, 93, 94
Demetria 106
De Divinatione 5, 124
De Natura Deorum 5, 125
Dido 52, 58
Diomedes 39, 53
Dione 9, 14, 16, 46
Dis 27, 30, 31
Dodona 9, 13, 16, 46
dolphin 14, 25

E

Egeria 46, 89, 98, 99
Eleusinian 56, 57, 64, 105
Elis 77
Elysian Fields, Elysium 28, 29, 31, 127
Eris 47
Eros 21, 50, 53, 60, 118, 119
Etna, Mount 60, 61, 128
Etruscans 1, 19, 36, 58, 72, 73, 81, 117, 125
Euripides 49, 69, 70, 110
Europa 21
Eurynome 17

F

fasces 88
Fates 5, 7, 16, 17, 26, 51
Fontus 74
Furies 5, 28

G

Gaia 2, 4, 5, 7, 9, 15, 20, 66, 97, 118
Gellius 76
Gorgons 116
Graces 17, 81
Gratian 33

H

Hadrian 42, 79, 80, 85, 86, 100
Hebe 17
Hecate 14, 44, 45, 57, 106, 116
Hector 72
Helen 47, 48
Helios 9, 30, 37, 41, 43, 44, 50, 60, 65, 116, 121
Heracles 9, 15, 22, 31, 53, 60, 61, 106, 110
Heraeum 81
Heraion 82
Herma, Hermaia 102, 128
Hermaphroditos 57
Hesiod 4, 5, 10, 11, 15, 16, 17, 21, 30, 46, 60, 63, 64, 67, 118
Hierapolis 86
hippocampi 26
Hippolytus 49, 120
Hippomenes 48, 67
Homer 16, 18, 23, 24, 25, 37, 46, 50, 60, 63, 64
Homeric Hymns 23, 30, 32, 33, 37, 41, 44, 46, 50, 53, 54, 55, 56, 57, 58, 61, 67, 68, 92, 128, 133
Horace 37, 65

I

Iasion 63, 64, 106
Iliad 18, 23, 24, 39, 53, 60
Ilithyia 24
Io 20, 21
Iphicles 22
Iris 41

J

Jason 16, 49, 106, 116
Jove 19
Juturna 74

K

Kronia 75

L

Latinus 117
Latin League 19, 98, 99, 123
Leda 47
Lethe 28
Leto 14, 17, 36, 37, 39, 94
Libera 66, 71, 107, 109, 110, 129
Liberalia 110
Libon 77
lictor 88

M

Macrobius 76, 103, 108, 112
Maenads 70
Magna Mater 48, 66, 67, 109
Maia 14, 17, 55, 58, 61, 103
Marsyas 39
Martial 76, 103
Medea 44, 49, 116
Medusa 25, 35, 115, 116
Melpomene 115

Menelaus 47, 48, 84
Mercuralia 102
Metis 8, 16, 34
Midas 40, 69
Minos 21, 28, 49, 117
Minotaur 49, 69, 117, 118
Mnemosyne 4, 17
Mount Ida 47
Muses 17, 61, 98, 115
Mycenae 47, 122

N

Naxos 49, 69, 118
Nemi 98, 99
Neptunalia 85, 86
Niobe 39, 44, 93, 94
Numa Pompilius 33, 73, 87, 98
numina 18, 125

O

Odysseus 26, 35, 91
Odyssey 50, 64, 84
Olympia 77, 82, 93, 102, 121
Olympus, Mount 13, 14, 18, 20, 23, 38, 46, 47, 50, 53, 55, 59, 60, 69, 70, 71
Opalia 76
Orcus 58
Orestes 96, 122
Orion 43
Orpheus 106, 119, 123
Orphic Hymns 8, 54, 65, 75, 101, 119
Ouranos 4, 5, 15, 118
Ovid 3, 20, 24, 30, 36, 40, 41, 57, 66, 67, 87, 91, 92, 94, 102, 112

P

Palladium 33, 89, 91
Pan 40, 56
Pandora 11, 12, 60
Pantheon 71, 85, 86
Paris 47, 48
Parnassus, Mount 92
Parthenos 36, 79, 90
Pasiphae 117
Peisistratos 79, 96
Peneus 38
Pericles 90
Persephone 14, 17, 30, 31, 44, 56, 57, 63, 64, 65, 66, 68, 71, 86, 105, 106, 123
Phaethon 40, 41
Pheidias (Phidias) 79, 90, 97, 121
Phlegethon 28
Phrygia, Phrygian 9, 39, 42, 67, 68, 119
pietas 58, 119, 125
Pindar 38
Pliny the Elder 93, 94, 97
Pliny the Younger 120
Plutonion, Plutonium 86, 105, 130
Plutus 27, 63, 64
Pollux 47
Polycleitus 81, 97
Polyphemus 25, 26
pomerium 84, 107
Pontifex Maximus 89, 121, 124
Praxiteles 65, 93, 102
Priam 38, 47, 49
Priapus 33
Prytaneion, Prytaneum 87, 105

Pygmalion 48
Pythia, Pythian 53, 70, 92, 93
Python 37, 92

Q

Quinquatrus 91, 92, 101
Quirinus 54, 81, 101, 112

R

Regia 89, 101, 124
Remus 54, 55, 100
Rhadamanthus 21, 28, 29
Romulus 24, 54, 55, 80, 100, 101, 112, 123, 124

S

Sabines 80, 112, 124
Salii 101
Samos 82, 102
Samothrace 106
Saturnalia 7, 76, 103, 108, 112
satyr 39, 40, 56
Scorpio 43
Selene 14, 43, 44, 45
Semele 17, 67, 68, 69
Seven Wonders of the World 79, 97, 120
Sibyl 41, 65, 94, 95
Silenus 69
Sirius 43
Socrates 32
Sounion 83, 84, 90
Sparta, Spartans 46, 47, 48, 96, 99
Stesichorus 47
Styx 17, 28, 40
Syrinx 40, 56

T

Tarquinius Pricus 81, 123
Tarquinius Superbus 41, 81, 94, 123
Tartarus 15, 26, 28, 29, 58
tauroctony 42, 95
Tellus 65, 106, 107
Thanatos 69
Thebes 39, 64, 70, 100
Themis 4, 16
Theogony 4, 7, 9, 11, 17, 53, 63, 67, 118
Theseus 49, 53, 69, 80, 116, 118
Thetis 18, 59, 69
Tiryns 82
Tisiphone 28
Titus Tatius 99, 112, 124
Triad 19, 23, 36, 61, 66, 71, 73, 81, 83, 107, 110
Troilius 38
Turms 58
Turnus 62, 117
Tyndareus 47

U

Uranus. *See* Ouranus

V

Vergil 24, 26, 27, 28, 51, 52, 58, 61, 62, 66, 94, 108
Vestal Virgins 33, 87, 88, 91, 122
Virbius 46, 98, 99
Volcanal 61, 103
Vulcanalia 61, 104

X

Xenia 76

BIBLIOGRAPHY

Beard, Mary, North, John and Price, Simon. *Religions of Rome*. Cambridge: Cambridge University Press, 1998.

Buxton, Richard. *The Complete World of Greek Mythology*. London: Thames & Hudson, 2004.

Carmody, Denise Lardner. *Women and World Religions*. New Jersey: Prentice Hall, 1989

Dumezil, Georges. *Archaic Roman Religion*. 2 vols. Trans. Philip Krapp. Chicago: The University of Chicago Press, 1970.

Goodison, Lucy. *Ancient Goddesses: The Myths and the Evidence*. London: British Museum Press. 1998.

Graves, Robert. *The Greek Myths*. Harmondsworth, England: Penguin Books, Ltd. 1955.

Harris, Stephen L and Platzner, Gloria. *Classical Mythology: Images and Insights*. New York: McGraw-Hill. 2003.

Lawrence, A. W. and Tomlinson, R.A. *Greek Architecture, 5th Edition*. London: Yale University Press. 1996.

Morford, Mark and Lenardon, Robert. *Classical Mythology, Seventh Edition*. Oxford: Oxford University Press. 2002.

Platner, Samuel Ball, (rev. Thomas Ashby). *Topographical Dictionary of Ancient Rome*. Oxford: Oxbow Books Ltd. 2002.

Scullard, H. H. *Festivals and Ceremonies of the Roman Republic*. London: Thames and Hudson, 1981.

Smith, William. *Dictionary of Greek and Roman Antiquities*, published in 1875: (accessed on LacusCurtius website).

Spaeth, Barbette Stanley. *The Roman Goddess Ceres*. Austin: University of Texas Press, 1996.

Stamper, John W. *The Architecture of Roman Temples: The Republic to the Middle Empire*. Cambridge University Press. 2005.

Ancient Sources:

Aeschylus, *Prometheus Bound*.

Apollodorus, *Bibliotheke*.

Aristophanes, *The Birds*.

Cassius Dio. *Roman History*.

Diodorus Siculus. *Bibliotheca Historica* (V, 3).

Ennius, Quintus. Fragmentary Works.

Euripides. *Bacchae*.

Gellius, Aulus. *Noctes Atticae*.

Herodotus. *Histories*.

Hesiod. *Theogony*.

Hippolytus. *Philosophumena*.

Homer. *Iliad* and *Odyssey*.

Homeric Hymns.

Horace. *Odes, Carmen Saeculare*.

Livy. *History of Rome*.

Macrobius. *Saturnalia*.

Martial. *Epigrams*.

Orphic Hymns.

Ovid. *The Metamorphoses*; *The Fasti*; *The Tristia*.

Pausanias. *Description of Greece*.

Petronius. *Satyricon*.

Philon of Byzantium, *De Septem Orbis Spectaculis*.

Pindar, *Odes*.

Pliny the Elder. *Natural History*.

Pliny the Younger. *Letters*.

Plutarch. *Lives of the Great Greeks and Romans*; *Moralia*.

Procopius of Caesarea. *History of the Wars*.

Propertius. *Elegiae*.

Vergil. *The Aeneid*.

Website References

http://www.drury.edu/ess/eastern/ChthonicHomeric.html

http://www.thelatinlibrary.com

http://penelope.uchicago.edu/Thayer/E/Roman/home.html

http://www.perseus.tufts.edu

http://www.sacred-texts.com/cla/hesiod/theogony.htm

http://sunsite.berkeley.edu/OMACL/Hesiod/hymns.html

http://www.ukans.edu/history/index/europe/ancient_rome/E/home.html